16|17

Taxonomy in the Classroom:

The Complete Guide

By Mike Gershon

Series Introduction

The 'How to...' series developed out of Mike's desire to share great classroom practice with teachers around the world. He wanted to put together a collection of books which would help professionals no matter what age group or subject they were teaching.

Each volume focuses on a different element of classroom practice and each is overflowing with brilliant, practical strategies, techniques and activities – all of which are clearly explained and ready-to-use. In most cases, the ideas can be applied immediately, helping teachers not only to teach better but to save time as well.

All of the books have been designed to help teachers. Each one goes out of its way to make educators' lives easier and their lessons even more engaging, inspiring and successful then they already are.

In addition, the whole series is written from the perspective of a working teacher. It takes account of the realities of the classroom, blending theoretical insight with a consistently practical focus.

The 'How to...' series is great teaching made easy.

Author Introduction

Mike Gershon is a teacher, trainer and writer. He is the author of over twenty books on teaching, learning and education, including a number of bestsellers, as well as the co-author of four others. Mike's online resources have been viewed and downloaded more than 2.8 million times by teachers in over 180 countries and territories. He writes regularly for the Times Educational Supplement and has created over 40 guides to different areas of teaching and learning as well as two online courses covering outstanding teaching and growth mindsets. Find out more, get in touch and download free resources at www.mikegershon.com

Training and Consultancy

Mike is an expert trainer whose sessions have received acclaim from teachers across England. Recent bookings include:

- *Growth Mindsets: Theory and Practice*

- *AFL Unlocked: Using Feedback and Marking to Raise Achievement*

- *Success in Linear Assessment: Strategies to Support Learners*

Mike also works as a consultant, advising on teaching and learning and creating bespoke materials for schools. Recent work includes:

- *Improving Literacy and Academic Language*

- *Growth Mindset Assemblies and Pastoral Support Materials*

If you would like speak to Mike about the services he can offer your school, please get in touch by email: mike@mikegershon.com

Acknowledgements

As ever I must thank all the fantastic colleagues and students I have worked with over the years, first while training at the Institute of Education, Central Foundation Girls' School and Nower Hill High School and subsequently while working at Pimlico Academy and King Edward VI School in Bury St Edmunds. Thanks also to Benjamin S. Bloom and the educators who worked together to create the taxonomy all those years ago.

Other Works from the Same Author

Available to buy now on Amazon:

How to use Differentiation in the Classroom: The Complete Guide

How to use Assessment for Learning in the Classroom: The Complete Guide

How to use Questioning in the Classroom: The Complete Guide

How to use Discussion in the Classroom: The Complete Guide

How to Teach EAL Students in the Classroom: The Complete Guide

How to be an Outstanding Trainee Teacher: The Complete Guide

How to use Bloom's Taxonomy in the Classroom: The Complete Guide

How to Manage Behaviour in the Classroom: The Complete Guide

More Secondary Starters and Plenaries

Secondary Starters and Plenaries: History

Teach Now! History: Becoming a Great History Teacher

The Growth Mindset Pocketbook (with Professor Barry Hymer)

How to be Outstanding in the Classroom: Raising achievement, securing progress and making learning happen

Also available to buy now on Amazon, the entire 'Quick 50' Series:

50 Quick and Brilliant Teaching Ideas

50 Quick and Brilliant Teaching Techniques

50 Quick and Brilliant Teaching Games

50 Quick and Easy Lesson Activities

50 Quick Ways to Help Your Students Secure A and B Grades at GCSE

50 Quick Ways to Help Your Students Think, Learn, and Use Their Brains Brilliantly

50 Quick Ways to Motivate and Engage Your Students

50 Quick Ways to Outstanding Teaching

50 Quick Ways to Perfect Behaviour Management

50 Quick Ways to Outstanding Group Work

50 Quick and Easy Ways to Prepare for Ofsted

50 Quick and Easy Ways Leaders can Prepare for Ofsted

50 Quick and Brilliant Ideas for English Teaching (with Lizi Summers)

50 Quick and Easy Ways to Build Resilience through English Teaching (with Lizi Summers)

50 Quick and Easy Ways to Outstanding English Teaching (with Lizi Summers)

Table of Contents

Introduction

Hello and welcome to *How to use Bloom's Taxonomy in the Classroom: The Complete Guide.* Since I first started teaching I have used the taxonomy as a major part of my planning, questioning, activities, differentiation and assessment. It is a brilliant tool. Versatile, flexible and easy to apply; founded on sound educational principles; and a natural promoter of challenge in any classroom.

Most teachers are familiar with the taxonomy; it is used ubiquitously as a basis for mark-schemes. Yet little attention has ever been given to what the taxonomy can really do for the practising teacher. The books currently out there are few and far between. Those that do exist tend to focus on the theory behind the taxonomy, giving no account of its practical use in the classroom.

This book changes all that.

It is the first attempt to systematically analyse the taxonomy with the classroom teacher in mind.

Through everything that follows, I have one guiding aim: to look at the taxonomy from the teacher's perspective and to show what it can do. In the pages ahead we travel far and wide, covering all the areas where the taxonomy is most useful.

Chapters 1 and 2 set the scene by providing an overview of the taxonomy's development and an explanation of how it works. Chapter 3 examines **knowledge and comprehension** in detail – the first two levels of the taxonomy – looking at what they are and how we can use them in practice.

Chapter 4 moves onto the next two levels – **application and analysis** – to repeat the trick. And we then go again, for a third and final time, in Chapter 5, where we turn to **synthesis and evaluation**.

At this point, the focus shifts. In the remainder of the book we examine how to apply the taxonomy in specific settings.

Chapter 6 looks at how to use the taxonomy to plan effective and challenging objectives and outcomes. Chapter 7 deals mainly with activities and, briefly, products. Chapter 8 looks at questioning, while Chapter 9 deals with assessment. Finally, Chapter 10 turns our attention to stretch and challenge.

Every chapter contains practical strategies, activities and techniques you can immediately apply to your own teaching. With that said, you can also adapt and modify the ideas as you see fit. And I am sure my suggestions will provoke ideas of your own. In this sense, the text is very much a starting point.

I hope you enjoy the book and find it useful. A collection of ready-to-use questions can be found in the appendix. These are based on keywords connected to comprehension, application, analysis, synthesis and evaluation. They can also be found in my book *How to use Questioning in the Classroom: The Complete Guide*. I include them here both for your benefit and out of a sense of completeness.

All that remains for me to say is read on and enjoy!

Chapter One – Bloom's Taxonomy: Background and Explanation

In this chapter we examine the origins of Bloom's Taxonomy of Educational Objectives, placing it in historical context, before briefly explaining how it works, what it tries to do and how it can help classroom teachers.

This is a complement to the following chapter, where we look in more depth at why the taxonomy works. Here, our aim is to set the scene; to provide a foundation from which we can move off and explore the practical application of the taxonomy to our teaching, marking and lesson planning.

The Origins of the Taxonomy

In the late 1940s and early 1950s, a series of conferences were held in America in which educators came together to try to improve communication around curriculum design and the nature of examinations. The period is notable for the wider transition in the West to what we now know as a post-war society. That is, one increasingly characterised by a changed relationship between citizens and the state, as well as one in which formal education played a greater role than ever before.

Perhaps the desire to formalise and, to some extent, systematise, the development of curricula and examinations reflected these changing norms. Certainly, the process would have been far less likely in the period immediately prior, defined first by the Great Depression and, subsequently, the Second World War.

With the growth of formal education and its increasing importance to industrialised society, the necessity for some form of codification of educational objectives became more pressing. A delineation of some type was inevitable, that it came in the form it did is as much down to the motives of those involved as it is to the wider historical processes.

Put another way, the years following the conclusion of the Second World War, seem a fecund period in which new ideas and developments about formal schooling could develop. Far more so than the decades preceding them.

The conferences were held between 1949 and 1953. Benjamin S. Bloom chaired the committee of educators who developed the taxonomy. He was an educational psychologist who studied at Pennsylvania State University and the University of Chicago.

The aim of the conferences was to codify the learning objectives educators set for their students. This codification came in the form of a taxonomy. A hierarchy of general processes which move from simple to complex in their make-up.

As a result of the conferences, a book was published in 1956. This was edited by Bloom and called: *Taxonomy of educational objectives: The classification of educational goals. Handbook I: Cognitive domain.*

A second book was published in 1964. This was called Handbook II: Affective domain. A third book was planned but never published. This was intended to deal with the psychomotor domain.

Most teachers are familiar only with the first of the taxonomies, concerning the cognitive domain. However, it is worth noting that the original attempts to classify learning objectives centred on a holistic view of education covering cognitive, affective and psychomotor processes. This indicates the educators who gathered at the conferences and who subsequently contributed to the books, Bloom among them, had an open and generous view of education – what it is and what it is for – rather than a reductive one.

Nonetheless, it is clear the taxonomy focussing on the cognitive domain gained real traction in the years following its development. This suggests educators and administrators found it useful in terms of classroom practice, curriculum design and the construction of exams. Further, it is this which most closely matches that which remains dominant in the discourse and practice surrounding schooling: the development of cognitive thought processes.

Few would deny the importance of the affective and psychomotor domains. But that the cognitive domain takes precedence in the majority of formal schooling is hard to deny.

From this point forwards then, while acknowledging the existence of the 1964 book, as well as the intention to produce a third dealing with the psychomotor domain, I will use the terms Bloom's Taxonomy and the taxonomy of the cognitive domain interchangeably. Whenever I talk about the taxonomy, I will be talking about the cognitive domain.

That is what the book is about. That is what we will focus on.

The reasoning is simple. Since its inception, it is this taxonomy which has had the greatest influence, this taxonomy which teachers are taught about during their training, and this taxonomy to which we all return again and again, to help us plan lessons, assessments and questions.

The influence of the taxonomy is not in doubt. It has become a cornerstone of teaching and learning. One of the most important foundations on which much of contemporary education is based. That it continues to be so influential is due in no small part to its simplicity. Through the categorisation and ordering of various connected processes, it provides teachers with a powerful tool through which to think about the learning their students do and the lessons they plan.

What the Taxonomy Is

This leads us nicely to the question of what the taxonomy is. Put bluntly, it is a hierarchy of processes ranging from the simple to the complex. To master those higher up you must first master those lower down. The processes to which it refers can be used in relation to almost any type of content, with the caveat that their use will be cognitive in nature (rather than affective or psychomotor). Here is the taxonomy:

Level 6 – Evaluation

Level 5 – Synthesis

Level 4 – Analysis

Level 3 – Application

Level 2 – Comprehension

Level 1 – Knowledge

Level 1, knowledge, is the simplest. Here we are concerned with recall, memory and knowing. This is about gaining information and making it a part of our minds, such that we can call on it and use it when thinking and doing at a later date. For example, we would expect students to know what a word means before expecting them to be able to do anything with that word.

Level 2, comprehension, is about understanding what we know. So, for example, I might be able to recall the definition of a word, but that does not necessarily mean that I would understand this definition or how the word might be used in the context of various different sentences. Comprehension centres on students being able to demonstrate an understanding of the facts they know (which they can remember).

Immediately, we see two important features inherent to the taxonomy.

The first is that, as said previously, there is a sense of development running through the levels. This is why the taxonomy promotes mastery learning. To be able to operate successfully at any given level, you must also be able to work successfully at the preceding level. Comprehension relies on prior knowledge, just as the ability to apply understanding rests on both comprehension and knowledge of the original facts.

Even though the taxonomy splits cognitive processes into a series of separate categories, there remains the sense that these processes do not exist independently of one another. Rather, they are interlinked and intertwined. The taxonomy is a delineation, yes, but so too is it akin to a building, in which the top levels can only exist if the bottom levels are already in place.

The second is that the taxonomy provides a framework which mirrors much of our experience of learning. This is to be hoped if it is to be effective. But let us just consider the point briefly. Think back to when you first encountered something with which you were not familiar. An idea perhaps, or a piece of information. Chances are that your natural inclination was to first try to understand what the thing in question was. And, to do this, you needed to know it – to be able to remember it.

Now, contrast this experience to a hypothetical individual who has no capacity to remember. Such an individual would not be able to understand any ideas or any information to which they were exposed because they would not be able to establish a starting point of remembrance from which to cast off. Their mind would not be able to assimilate the knowledge necessary to lead to understanding. This further demonstrates how the taxonomy reflects the lived experience of learning. (As a side point, our hypothetical individual would probably struggle ever to become a person as well, given as how our sense of self rests in large part on the ability to remember things concerning who we are and what we have done.)

After comprehension we have level 3, application. Here, we are concerned with how a student can take their knowledge and understanding of something and apply it in novel (and sometimes familiar) situations. The aim is to use the foundations which have been established to deal with things with which we are presented. In the classroom, this often involves students answering questions or solving problems once they have secured a basic level of understanding concerning a given topic.

Level 4, analysis, takes things a step further. It involves us being able to take apart that with which we are presented in order to show relationships, motives, causes, connections and ways of working. To be able to analyse something, we need to be able to apply that which we know and understand. If we haven't mastered, at least to some degree, the process of application, we will find it hard to effectively analyse that with which we are presented.

For example, we might ask a group of students to analyse how an engine works. To do this, they would need to examine the engine in detail, looking at how the parts connect together, looking at what causes what and how the different parts influence and interact with one another. Without a prior knowledge and understanding of engines and engine parts, a knowledge and understanding which students feel confident applying to different situations, this task will be very difficult. Students might be able to point to how things within the engine connect or affect each other – they might even be able to describe this in some rudimentary way – but without a degree of mastery over the underlying facts and principles, they will struggle to accurately analyse the structure of the engine to any meaningful degree.

Once again, this illustrates the way in which the levels of the taxonomy are interlinked and how successful mastery relies on firm foundations.

Moving on, we see that level 5 is synthesis. This involves the creation of that which is new. It could be completely new or it could be a development of something already existing. In this sense, the category covers a wide range of cognitive processes. In the context of analysis, the intellectual development here stems from the fact that a student needs to be able to effectively analyse the structure and make-up of a given item if they are to create something which reflects this, utilises it or goes beyond it.

Let us continue with our engine example to illustrate the point.

Having successfully analysed the structure of the engine, students are now asked to design an improvement to make the engine more efficient.

The word 'design' here signifies that an act of synthesis is being requested. And that act cannot be successfully completed unless students are first able to analyse the structure of the existing engine. This is because any improvement which they design will have to take account of that which exists already. Thus we see the central feature of all synthesis-base cognitive acts: the movement from what is to what could be.

Successful synthesis relies on an analytical understanding of what has come first. Another example further demonstrates the point. If we ask a student to create an argument supporting the abolition of the death penalty in those countries where it remains in force, we are expecting that students have some degree of analytical understanding of what constitutes an argument as well as the idea surrounding the death penalty itself. If students are unable to analyse why the death penalty still exists and why many argue that it should not, then they will not have the tools necessary with which to construct their own argument regarding its abolition.

Once again, the metaphor of a building is helpful. It is easier to build on firm foundations than it is on shaky ones. In the latter case, we are severely limited in the scope of what we can do. And, crucially, there is a much higher likelihood that our edifice will fall down if it is put under any sort of pressure.

This is exactly what happens in the classroom, though not necessarily to bad effect.

For example, a student who has failed to grasp the way in which our engine works may produce a design which, when put into practice, quickly fails. Now, this would demonstrate to us as the teacher that the student does not have a sufficient grasp of the engine's structure to create a successful improvement. But, it would also give the student an important learning opportunity. When played out, either in practice or through a model, they would see the failure of their design and then be compelled to ask: Why did it go wrong?

To answer the question they would need to return to the drawing board and compare what they did with what they know about the engine. However, this knowledge would now be supplemented by the knowledge of their design's failure! From here they can begin to deduce further information about the engine's structure, by comparing what they thought they understood with what actually happened when they tried to build on their understanding.

Exceptional application of Bloom's Taxonomy by teachers therefore involves the creation of an environment in which students are encouraged to see their mistakes as essential steps on the path to mastery.

A brief detour to reinforce this point before we turn to level 6, evaluation.

When developing the electric lightbulb, Thomas Edison went through hundreds of iterations with a team of workers. Each attempt was a failure. But each one provided an insight into why success had not been forthcoming.

Eventually, Edison and his team were able to produce a working lightbulb. They had mastered the process.

We might look at this as an incessant, repetitive journey between analysis and synthesis. Working with incomplete knowledge, Edison and his team continually tried to create something based on their analysis of what they did know and understand. Each failure indicated the incompleteness of their analysis. Therefore, on each occasion, they had to return to this and see what they could glean by comparing what they did know and understand with the information provided by the failure.

We can safely assume that, by the end of the process and the creation of the working prototype, the analytical understanding possessed by Edison and his team was far in advance of that with which they had started. And it was this, in large part, that would have enabled them to create (synthesise) a solution to their problem.

This process can be put in simpler terms: trial and error.

Invariably, engaging in synthesis serves to enhance our analytical understanding because the things we create are less perfect than we expect them to be.

We will return to this idea in Chapter Six, when we look at synthesis and evaluation in more detail.

Now let us complete our initial journey through the taxonomy by looking at level 6, evaluation.

To be able to assess, judge or rank an item or series of items successfully, we need to know what the things in question are, understand our own knowledge of them, be able to apply this to different situations, be able to analyse the nature of that which is in question and, to mark the success of this, be able to construct new developments. Only with this prerequisite knowledge and understanding will we be able to provide a thorough, nuanced judgement. Or, to put it another way, a masterful one.

A few points arise from this.

First, evaluation, like the preceding levels, can be done usefully without being perfect. If, for example, we ask students to assess whether it would be a good idea to ban homework, we can reasonably expect them to give an interesting, relatively well-conceived response, even if this judgement would not be marked by absolute mastery of the topic. Similarly, we might expect that all students in a class could reach a level of evaluation regarding a given topic, but that the extents and quality of this evaluation will vary depending on the prior knowledge and understanding of the students in question. A student who knows more and understands more has far more on which they can call in order to make a judgement than a student who knows less and understands less.

In the case of the latter student, judgement might be difficult to achieve, it might be general and vague, or it might rest on knowledge and understanding taken from somewhere else (as, for example, when a student attempts to rely on their knowledge of a related topic in order to make a judgement about the present topic, of which they know less).

The world of medicine will help us to illustrate this point.

Imagine we have a minor ailment. We attend our local GP's surgery and see the doctor. The doctor examines us to assess the nature and extent of our complaint. In so doing, they call on their extensive yet general knowledge and understanding of medicine.

Two paths may follow. In the first case, the doctor's judgement proves correct. They prescribe a course of treatment and, within a week, we feel much better. Here, the doctor's knowledge and understanding (levels 1-5) are sufficient to warrant a successful, masterly diagnosis (assessment) of the problem, along with a concomitant treatment.

In the second case, we return to the doctor after a week and tell them there has been no change in our condition. The treatment has had no effect. The doctor might tell us to persist a while longer, or they might refer us to a specialist.

Why? Because a specialist possesses a depth of knowledge and understanding concerning the area in question which is far in excess of that required to be a successful general practitioner. The GP, having made the best assessment of which they are capable, given the knowledge and understanding they possess, acknowledges that someone with greater expertise would be better placed to accurately assess the nature of the problem. The specialist is that person. Because they have chosen to specialise, they have been able to focus their mind on a particular area, gaining an expert's knowledge and understanding which, in turn, allows them to make expert judgements.

Of course, it does not follow that their judgements will always be correct. But it does follow that they are better placed to make correct judgements.

This vignette illustrates why effective evaluation rests on mastery of prior knowledge and understanding as well as the fact that effective evaluation is a continuum along which different students can sit at different times.

In short, you do not have to have complete mastery of all the preceding levels to give a judgement, but the greater your mastery, the better your judgement is likely to be.

This demonstrates that not all judgements need to be masterful but that better judgements will be closer towards mastery then poorer judgements.

I have stressed this point, along with that about synthesis and trial and error, because some may argue that the higher levels of the taxonomy are inaccessible to less able students. I disagree.

My reasoning is not that every student will be able to synthesise and evaluate to the same extent. Clearly they won't (as has been implicitly argued above). But all students will be able to access synthesis and evaluation to some extent, using their prior knowledge and understanding to create new things or pass judgements. These may not work or may face significant criticism. But so what? That's good! Because it is in this erring that learning takes place.

And that is why I would suggest that we think of the challenge inherent in Bloom's Taxonomy as open to all students; with that challenge being met and experienced in different ways.

For example, a very able student may produce a detailed evaluative summary of a piece of work they have created. This is challenging in itself and we could further challenge them by questioning the validity of certain aspects of their judgement.

A less-able student may produce a quite general assessment of their work which belies their limited understanding. However, coming up with the judgement will still have been a challenge. And we can further push their thinking by asking them questions which cause them to revisit their knowledge and understanding at the level of application or analysis. This helps them to sharpen their abilities, leading to a revised judgement which rests on a deeper and more detailed knowledge and understanding of the topic in question.

This leads us to our final point, which echoes something we said earlier about synthesis.

Evaluation can produce a useful feedback loop, just the same as the synthesis-analysis loop outlined above. If we pass judgement and then find that the judgement does not hold, does not fit with information of which we were previously unaware or which we overlooked, or is challenged on grounds we had not considered, then once again we have information on which we can act to improve matters.

In the classroom, a failed judgement is not a failure in itself. It is only a failure if we seek to do nothing with it. If, on the other hand, we use the information provided to go back and look again, then we are learning.

For example, a student assesses Ted Hughes's use of imagery in a given poem. During the lesson we read their judgement and pose a question which challenges them to analyse an aspect of the poem they have overlooked. This question is based on our own analysis of the student's judgement. An analysis which has spotted their failure to take account of something important. By going back to re-examine the thing in question, the student further develops their analytical understanding of the poem. This leads, in turn, to a higher quality judgement second time around.

The example demonstrates how evaluation can be the basis for a trial and error feedback loop, just as synthesis can. You might even argue that, in many cases, the two levels are intertwined (we create and evaluate at the same time, using the latter as part of the former, see where we went wrong and then return to analysis before trying again).

Mastery Learning

In offering a basic overview of what the taxonomy is and how the different levels interconnect, I have regularly referred to the idea of mastery learning. This concept is one on which the taxonomy rests and it is worth our while attending to the idea separately before we move on.

If we master something we become expert in it. This expertise makes itself known through how we exercise our knowledge and understanding of the thing in question. We can do so with a high level of skill, precision and accuracy.

Stevie Wonder is a master of the piano. Lionel Messi has a mastery of football. Dame Judi Dench is a masterful actor.

In each case, mastery gives the individual in question prowess in the field of which they are expert. They make excellent judgements, adapt themselves to different situations with ease, can improvise highly effectively, can alter, change and modify things to suit their own interpretation, are able to make that which is difficult look simple, and can go beyond what exists to do things in a way which is resolutely their on – neither imitative nor mechanical but superior to those with whom they share, in this case, a profession.

Such expertise might be thought of as the pinnacle of mastery.

Yet, mastery can also be thought of as something less profound. Maybe I learn a new word during the course of my day, use this word in the weeks which follow, check its meaning, try it out in different situations and then, a few months later, find myself well placed to call on the word in a skilful manner when speaking or writing.

I have developed a mastery of this word. I know what it means and understand when it is most appropriately used. The word can be called on to my satisfaction.

Here we see two different senses of mastery learning. The first involves becoming a master of an area to which we dedicate ourselves. The second involves mastering something to which we have been exposed or about which we want to learn. That mastery may evolve and develop over time, but a basic mastery can be seen through how we are able to manipulate the thing in question.

It is this second form of mastery with which we are mostly concerned in the classroom. We will no doubt come across certain students in our careers who exhibit or seek mastery of the first type, but these will likely be rare.

The second form, in which mastery learning refers to one's ability to fully know and understand a skill or piece of content, such that it can be used effectively and with ease, is something to which we can help all our students to aim.

Bloom's Taxonomy promotes this type of learning because by moving up the levels of the taxonomy any individual can become more knowledgeable, more skilled and develop a better understanding of that about which they are seeking to learn. This is for the reasons outlined above, concerning the structure of the taxonomy, the relative increase in complexity attributed to each successive level and the manner in which the levels interlink.

When we plan lessons or schemes of work, we can use the taxonomy to help us achieve our wider aim of maximising progress. We can do this safe in the knowledge that the structure and application of the taxonomy echoes this objective. Mastery learning is contiguous with maximising progress. If students are making great progress they are mastering ideas and information. If they are mastering ideas and information then, in so doing, they are making great progress.

A Framework for Teaching, Learning and Assessment

For all the reasons above, the taxonomy provides an excellent framework for teaching, learning and assessment. That this is the case can be seen from the extent to which it underpins these practices in many parts of the world.

The taxonomy is inherently progressive. By progressive I mean the levels contain an increasing degree of challenge. This means lessons and assessments using the taxonomy can be quickly and easily made challenging for all learners.

On the flipside, if a teacher ignores the taxonomy when doing their planning, they make life much harder for themselves. And they increase the chance that what they produce will not rest upon an increasing degree of challenge.

The taxonomy is also simple. We can apply it across the curriculum and across the age-groups. In the first case, we simply alter the content. In the second case, we alter the extent of what we are asking students to do, as well as the content.

To get a sense of the ubiquity of the taxonomy, take a look at the mark-schemes and assessment objectives provided by any examining body in almost any subject. Invariably you will see the mark of Bloom's Taxonomy, visible to a greater or lesser extent, but nearly always there, in the background, ordering and underpinning the process of assessment.

Throughout this opening chapter I have implied through my explanation of what the taxonomy is that I believe it to be extremely useful when it comes to teaching, learning and assessment. That I have chosen to devote an entire book to the topic further illustrates the fact.

In the chapters which follow I will first provide a little more analysis of why I believe the taxonomy works so well and how we can best apply it, in general sense, in the classroom. Then, and for the majority of the book, we will look at practical examples of how to use it effectively.

Before we move on to this, there is one last thing to which we must attend.

Subsequent Developments

The taxonomy is not immune from criticism. None of this refutes the central argument the taxonomy makes, or the process of categorising and ordering cognitive processes which it entails. However, there are three points we should consider here.

First, some have argued the taxonomy is not, in fact, a properly constructed taxonomy. This is because there is no systemic rationale of construction. While this may be true, the criticism does not detract from the taxonomy's efficacy, nor its usefulness in systematising educational objectives and providing educators with a clear lens through which to see teaching, learning and assessment.

The taxonomy was revised in 2001 by Anderson et al. In their work, the issue of whether it was properly constructed or not was addressed. This also leads us to our second point. In the revision, it was suggested that analysis, synthesis and evaluation should be seen side-by-side rather than in a hierarchy. Personally, I do not find this adaptation particularly useful. While it may provide a more systematic taxonomy, it reduces its power as a tool on which the classroom teacher can call.

As to whether the top three levels should be seen in parallel, or whether, as some have argued, synthesis and evaluation should be swapped over, so that the former is at the peak of the taxonomy, I leave it to you to judge. For the purposes of this book, I will refer to the original taxonomy, as outlined above, and, while privileging evaluation over synthesis, suggest that the top two levels can be thought of as interchangeable.

Third and finally, many have argued that the taxonomy separates out processes which, in reality, do not exist independently of one another. Thought, they say, is an inherently complex process made up of disparate elements at any one time, meaning that it is too simplistic to say that the six levels can exist in separation.

I agree with this and, indeed, have made mention of the point in the analysis above. I am sure you agree with it as well. After all, each one of us has experience of thought and it is hard to argue that it ever does echo the neat delineations of the taxonomy.

But such criticism rather misses the point.

The taxonomy is a practical tool for teachers. By dividing up processes, ordering and systematising them, it makes the teacher's life easier and gives them a powerful device through which to plan teaching, learning and assessments. So, yes, the criticism is fair. But, no, it shouldn't cause us to cast the taxonomy aside.

For teaching is a practical business, and it is in the practical arena that the taxonomy finds its greatest use. And for more on this, read on...

Chapter Two – An Analysis of Why the Taxonomy Works

In this chapter my aims are as follows:

i.   To build on the initial analysis of the taxonomy provided in Chapter One.
ii. To demonstrate how the taxonomy reflects the structure of thought.
iii. To explain how its application in the classroom enhances the teaching and learning process.

Half a Century

We begin in the past, more than half a century ago. As we noted at the start of the previous chapter, the taxonomy was first conceived in the years following World War Two. The book covering the cognitive domain was published in 1956. This is some time ago. Fifty-nine years as I write.

This throws up two questions. First, why does the taxonomy remain in use? Second, is it not time we had something reflecting the changed world in which we live today?

Setting aside the 2001 revision of the taxonomy mentioned at the end of the last chapter, let us answer each question in turn.

Things tend to remain in use for a number of different reasons, some good and some bad. There is inertia, familiarity, laziness, the lack of a better alternative, vested interests, stability, conservatism, gradual refinement, and continued efficacy.

I would argue that it is the last of these which underpins the continued use of Bloom's Taxonomy today, nearly sixty years after its print debut. That the taxonomy retains a high degree of efficacy can be shown by turning to our second question.

While society has changed significantly since the taxonomy was first put together, these changes have not necessitated or caused a change in the underlying structures through which we think. And it these structures – processes – which the taxonomy sought to define, order and systematise.

Today, we see the processes applied in ways which could have barely been imagined sixty years ago: the computer programmer who creates (synthesis) a new piece of software; the brain surgeon who assesses (evaluates) the usefulness of a neuroscience research paper; the student who comes to comprehend the importance and characteristics of newly-discovered sub-atomic particles.

In each case, the content is new and previously unknown, representing an extension of the range and scope of human knowledge and understanding. But the processes through which individuals engage with that content remain the same. Evaluation is as relevant today as it was sixty years ago. It retains the prominent position it previously occupied in our thinking. The passage of time does not erode this.

Why is this the case? A few tentative answers suggest themselves.

First, cognitive processes are constitutive of the structures of thought on which our minds rest. This means that they are both total and unchanging. To have a previously unknown cognitive process would be akin to seeing a colour which falls beyond the range of human perception. The processes which underpin our thinking are coterminous with the extents of our thinking. They cannot be surpassed.

Second, the processes can, arguably, be logically derived from the starting point of learning, which itself is a biological function of human beings. That starting point is memory (as we noted earlier, when considering the impossibility of learning – as well as self-hood – for an individual without memory). Through memory the infant child can come to associate certain things with other things. This marks the beginning of learning. That is, of coming to remember what the world is like, how it relates to us, how we relate to it and so forth.

As human beings we have over many thousands of years taken advantage of the evolutionary adaptation of memory to develop culture. Culture is a world which sits atop the physical world we inhabit. It is a world of meaning which cannot exist independently of human beings. This is because any physical manifestations or carriers of culture require at least some degree of decoding if their meaning is to be conveyed. Included in the world of culture is language, the central way through which we communicate and pass on information.

Language allows us to store far more information than would otherwise be possible. Literacy further increases our advantage (contrast the extent of a literate person's intellectual reach and that of someone who is illiterate).

So the infant child comes to know language as well as experience. Language then gives them a means through which to name experience. Comprehending is derived from knowing. This is because when we come to know things we come to remember them and, through that remembrance, are in a position to compare them. This can be as simple as sitting two things next to each other in our minds. Again, only possible because we can first remember the things in question.

Sitting things next to each other is perhaps the simplest way to begin building on knowledge. If we remember that a cat is a cat and a dog is a dog, we can think of the cat and the dog and, in so doing, recognise that they are two different things. This recognition is an act of comprehension, of understanding. It is the beginning of coming to understand the extents of the thing remembered, as well as its relationship to other things remembered.

Once we have some form of comprehension we are able to remember this (thus understanding becomes a fact or piece of knowledge, forming a part of our internal experience; my understanding and your understanding of a cat may be similar but they are not one and the same thing). We can then remember this comprehension in new situations and, again, make an act of comparison. So, for example, I might encounter a creature which looks like a cat, only a lot bigger. I apply my understanding of cats to this in order to see if the thing in question is a cat. I decide that it is only partially like a cat but also notice that it fits with my existing understanding of bigness. So I term it a big cat(!).

When we can remember a thing, comprehend it and apply it, with all of this predicated on memory of the thing in question, the higher order processes (analysis, synthesis and evaluation) naturally follow.

We can analyse what we know and what we come across, basing this analysis on the existing understanding we possess. The process of analysis can perhaps be thought of as a critical application to a series of elements, as opposed to a general application to a situation as a whole. And we have stressed the relationship and derivation between analysis, synthesis and evaluation in the previous chapter.

In summary, and this explication has been both brief and partial in seeking to make the point, the general processes defined by the taxonomy can be logically derived from the starting point of being able to remember and of exercising this capacity in the context of a society which possesses language.

Much more could be said on this topic, though I leave it for another time.

Here we can say simply that the taxonomy remains in use so many years after its construction because it retains its efficacy. This efficacy stems from the fact that it still reflects the thinking we do as well as the general structure of our thought.

Delineating and Defining Processes

We move now to think about what the delineation and defining of cognitive processes means in the context of the classroom. What are the implications, we are asking, for teaching and learning?

First, let me flesh out the bare bones of the taxonomy by providing a non-exhaustive list of keywords connected to each of the levels. This will help us to think about each of the categories rather more clearly:

Knowledge:

Arrange, Define, Describe, List, Match, Memorise, Name, Order, Quote, Recognise, Recall, Repeat, Reproduce, Restate, Retain.

Comprehension:

Characterise, Classify, Complete, Describe, Discuss, Establish, Explain, Express, Identify, Illustrate, Recognise, Report, Relate, Sort, Translate.

Application:

Apply, Calculate, Choose, Demonstrate, Dramatize, Employ, Implement, Interpret, Operate, Perform, Practise, Role-Play, Sketch, Solve, Suggest.

Analysis:

Analyse, Appraise, Categorize, Compare, Contrast, Differentiate, Discriminate, Distinguish, Examine, Experiment, Explore, Investigate, Question, Research, Test.

Synthesis:

Combine, Compose, Construct, Create, Devise, Design, Formulate, Hypothesise, Integrate, Merge, Organise, Plan, Propose, Synthesise, Unite.

Evaluation:

Appraise, Argue, Assess, Critique, Defend, Evaluate, Examine, Grade, Inspect, Judge, Justify, Rank, Rate, Review, Value.

Some words could reasonably be placed in more than one category. This reflects the fact that the words in question have multiple meanings, as well as the interrelated nature of thinking. (Please note, you can also find these lists at the start of Chapters 3, 4 and 5).

Looking over the list we can see that each collection of words points to a range of ways in which the general process can play out in practical terms. This is important.

The different words exist for good reason. They refer to different things. While these things may be similar and, on occasion, almost identical, the words remain in currency because they serve specific purposes.

Take defend and critique, for example. These both involve us engaging in a process of assessment. In each case, though, the assessment is in a different direction. To defend something we need to assess its strengths and weaknesses, marshal these in a way that puts the best case forward for the thing in question, and marry this up with criticisms of the alternatives. To critique something we have to work in the opposite direction. Our aim is more heavily proscribed. We are drawing out the weaknesses of the thing in question and, while we may do this in part by making unfavourable comparisons to strengths found in other places, we will most likely focus on the negative things associated with the object of our assessment.

Compare and differentiate offer another example, here taken from the category of analysis. When comparing two things our aim is to see to what extent they are similar and, by extension, different. Any acknowledgement of the degree of similarity is, at least implicitly, an acknowledgement of the degree of difference as well (if we say that two things are roughly similar it follows that they are not particularly dissimilar). If our aim is to differentiate, we focus our analysis on picking out the things which are different – which separate out the things in question. We might call on a degree of comparison to do this, but the act itself will not be the same as comparison, because our aim is firmly bound up with accentuating and cataloguing the differences on view.

These examples illustrate how each category of the taxonomy is home to a range of variations on a theme. These variations exist because they refer to different things. Put together, they make up the wider category. Individually, they represent cases within each category.

When it comes to teaching and learning, we find ourselves at a significant advantage if we are familiar with a range of keywords for each general process. This allows us to plan objectives, outcomes, activities and questions more precisely.

Consider how limited our scope would be if we only ever referred to the six category titles: knowledge, comprehension, application, analysis, synthesis and evaluation. It would be like trying to create an intricate carving using only a hammer and a single chisel; our job would be far harder than if we had a wider range of tools at our disposal, allowing us to differentiate, specialise and make thoughtful choices based on the particular part of our work in which we were engaged at any one time.

Synthesis is the category in which this is perhaps most apparent. The word is unwieldy at classroom level. It also possesses a rather striking chemistry connotation (this is not a bad thing in itself, it merely serves to indicate the word is not that closely tied to the set of words which fall under its umbrella – particularly create – and which we seek to promote in the classroom).

Familiarising yourself with the categories of the taxonomy, their order and their meaning is therefore helpful. As is getting to know a range of keywords for each level. This will give you greater scope with which to act when applying the taxonomy to your planning, teaching and marking, as well as to the construction of any assessments.

Cross-Curricular and Cross-Age-Group Applicability

The taxonomy is a flexible, adaptable tool we can apply across the curriculum and to a range of different age-groups. This is another one of its strengths. As stated above, it reflects the structure of our thought and is organised in a manner echoing the increasing complexity through which we can understand a particular thing.

It follows that the taxonomy can be applied to different topics; in any case, the wider process remains the same. Students will be asked to engage with the content in question through the different processes contained within the taxonomy.

We might plan a lesson looking at sheep, at bulldozers, at nuclear physics or at the poetry of A. E. Houseman. In all these cases, we could apply the taxonomy. The content does not limit its efficacy. For example, we could explain to students what sheep are, then ask them to pick out examples of sheep from a picture-book of animals before asking them to explain how they know that a sheep is a sheep and not a cow. Similarly, we could ask students to read through Houseman's A Shropshire Lad, to familiarise themselves with the poems therein, to explain the meaning of a given poem and then to explain how they might go about identifying whether or not an unclaimed poem had a high chance of being one of Houseman's or not.

These two examples illustrate how the complexity of the content we are teaching tends to define the degree of complexity inherent in the relative cognitive processes. It is less complex to know what a sheep is than it is to know Houseman's poems, yet both acts still fall into the category of knowledge.

Equally, it is less demanding to explain why a sheep is not a cow than it is to explain why an unmarked poem may or may not have been written by Houseman.

And it is in this summary that we can witness why the taxonomy can be applied to different age-groups as well as to different topics.

The processes delineated by the taxonomy can be engaged in to varying extents. Evaluation for a seven year old is not the same as evaluation for a sixteen year old, yet the relationship between application, analysis and evaluation as regards a specific piece of content remains the same.

This means that we should see the taxonomy as being connected to Bruner's concept of the spiral curriculum. That idea posits that students return to key concepts and ideas at different points on their educational journey, each time meeting them at a more advanced stage of development. Hence, a student may meet the concept of change multiple times in every year of their school life. But each subsequent meeting will be at a level higher than the last – as if the students is journeying up a spiral staircase, revisiting points they have previously seen but at a higher level than was previously the case.

In terms of the taxonomy, students are capable of climbing the six levels throughout most of their school career (with the caveat that abstract thought tends not to be sufficiently developed in the earliest years to make the higher levels accessible) but the extent of their proficiency, the depth of their understanding and the complexity of the content with which they are dealing will grow with them, as they develop.

This leads us to that conclusion that the taxonomy can be applied across the curriculum and when working with the majority of age-groups.

Building Blocks of Understanding

It seems natural to think of knowledge in terms of building blocks. We learn facts and information. These form the foundations of our thought. As we grow older we learn more, leading to knowledge which is wider, deeper and broader.

Understanding feels a little different. Seeing it as building blocks is not quite so easy. It does not have that same sense of discreteness as knowledge seems to possess. When we know something we know it.

It is our knowledge. It can be boxed off and specified. 1066. Richard Of York Gave Battle In Vain.

Understanding is applied, more continuous. To say we understand something means we know it and we know about it. The definition is not as clear-cut. There is more room for interpretation – literally as well as figuratively.

When it comes to teaching though, it can at times be helpful for us to conceive of understanding as a series of building blocks in a similar vein to knowledge. This entails us seeing understanding as being constituted of a series of separate elements which can be set apart, viewed in isolation and worked on accordingly by our learners.

When we take such an approach we can plan activities and lesson segments which focus on different aspects of understanding; the different building blocks to which we have just alluded.

Now, there is a qualification to add. What I am not saying is that understanding is constituted of a set of separate blocks. This seems unlikely, and to come to even a tentative answer on the topic would require a great deal more work. Rather, I am saying that *it can be useful for us as teachers to think about understanding in this way.*

This is because it gives us a means through which to break down a large and potentially impenetrable idea (understanding) into a series of elements we can put to practical use.

I'm sure you've guessed the rest of my argument already!

Bloom's Taxonomy does this for us.

By dividing thought up into six categories, it helps us to see understanding as a series of blocks which can be placed one after the other.

This takes us back to the metaphor of building a house we used in the first chapter.

Coming to understand ideas and information is a bit like building a house from the ground up. We lay foundations, add to these, and keep going until we have produced the complete package. Arguably, this is how we can view our students' understanding when applying the taxonomy to our lessons and across schemes of work.

For example, in a particular lesson we might start off by having students learn new information and then answer questions about this (knowledge and comprehension). Next, they apply their learning to a set of problems and analyse the results of their application. Finally, in the last section of the lesson, we ask them to assess the quality of the information at issue in light of certain criteria.

Examining this exemplar through the building blocks approach, we can imagine that each subsequent activity or lesson segment, all of which are based on an upwards movement through the taxonomy, is an additional building block of understanding being laid down for the benefit of our students.

Personally, I find this approach helpful. It is a useful, practical model through which to build pace, challenge and progress into any lesson.

Facilitating Challenge

We can now think about challenge in more depth and, specifically, how the taxonomy helps teachers to facilitate challenge in lessons.

Challenge means asking students to go beyond what they can currently do.

It means students facing greater demands on their cognitive capacities than would be the case if they were able to switch off and glide through a lesson without really exerting themselves.

It means the teacher has considered what current level of skill, knowledge and understanding students possess, and then considered how they can push them to develop these.

If we are being challenged, it means we are working at or near the edge of our abilities. It is through this that we come to push back the frontier, enlarging the scope of what we can do.

Challenge is intimately tied up with trial and error and making mistakes. If we are trying to do something we cannot do yet, we will make some mistakes along the way. Indeed, we will need to make mistakes if we want to learn enough to take us forward (and, it could be argued, a challenge is not enough of a challenge if we can meet it quickly and with relatively little error).

Great teaching sees the teacher maintaining a high level of challenge throughout their lessons. Doing this means students learn more and make more progress for the reasons stated above. Yet this is not easy.

For one thing, finding the means through which to keep stretching the thinking of the students we teach is time-consuming and intellectually demanding. For another, maintaining a consistently accurate knowledge of where our students are at in terms of their understanding (and what we need to do if we are to challenge them) requires rigorous elicitation and analysis of information regarding student learning.

The taxonomy is a tool which, through its application, allows us to circumvent both these problems.

We can begin by considering how we go about stretching students' thinking.

Trying to come up with new strategies and techniques on a regular basis is hard to achieve. Even developing your own suite of measures over a period of time isn't easy. But, the taxonomy provides us with everything we need in an easy-to-use, ready-to-apply format.

As we have seen, each level of the taxonomy is more challenging than the last. Even if we take synthesis and evaluation as being on the same level, it still stands that these two processes are more complex than analysis, which is more complex than application and so on.

Any time we find ourselves in a situation where we want to stretch and challenge our students' thinking, we can turn to the taxonomy for help. Heading to the top two levels, we find a range of command words (see earlier) which can form the basis of questions or tasks. That these will be challenging goes without saying. They represent the most complex of the cognitive processes and, therefore, ask students to engage in more challenging cognitive work connected to the topic of study.

Of course, it may be that challenge for one student is not the same as challenge for another student. This is not an issue, though. If, for example, we pose an evaluative challenge to a particular student and it quickly becomes apparent that this is a step too far, we can scale matters back and pose an analytical challenge instead. That we know this is simpler than the initial task but still challenging stems from our knowledge of the taxonomy. Again we see the practical benefits which spring from familiarity with the model.

Coming now to the second point, regarding the need to consistently understand where students are at and what therefore constitutes a challenge for them, we again find the taxonomy to be of use. This has been intimated in the previous paragraph, where we noted how to scale back challenge in accordance with the response it draws, moving down the levels of the taxonomy as we do.

The opposite applies as well. If we plan an activity based around comprehension and quickly see that most of our students are racing through it more quickly than we expected, we simply turn to the taxonomy and introduce a sub-task or challenge question based on application and/or analysis. Immediately the level of challenge has been raised, with little effort required on our part, but with this being in direct response to the information we have elicited about students' present understanding.

Our final point here concerns diagnosis. By diagnosis we mean the diagnosis of student knowledge and understanding. In other words, using questions to work out where students are at. This is one of the primary ways through which we gain knowledge of our students' understanding.

During a lesson, we can test and probe student understanding by asking questions based on the different levels of Bloom's Taxonomy. Doing this helps us to see the extent of our students' understanding and to identify the point in the taxonomy they have reached, in relation to the content. They may be straddling two levels, or they may be demonstrating proficiency at one level in relation to one aspect of the content but not the other aspects. Whatever we find – whether it indicates a uniform level of understanding or not – we can use this information as the basis for our subsequent interventions which, once again, will be predicated on an application of the taxonomy.

So, for example, we might ask a middle-ability student a series of application and analysis questions. This reveals they have fully comprehended the lesson content and are well-placed to try some high-level problem-solving. Armed with this knowledge we realise the next step is to set the student up with a creative or evaluative task – and to let them know they might fail at first, but that they should use this as an opportunity to further develop their understanding before trying again.

Framing Assessments

We come now to our last section, after which we will look at practical applications of the taxonomy in the remaining chapters. Here I want to say a few things about how the taxonomy can be used to frame assessments and why it is effective when used in this way.

Assessment aims at establishing the present status of a student's knowledge and understanding. It does this by eliciting information from the student and comparing this information to a set of criteria. Assessment can be informal, such as when we ask a question, gain a response and compare this to our existing knowledge and expectations concerning the students we teach. Assessment can also be formal, such as when we ask students to sit down and take a test, which we then mark, comparing their answers to a set of criteria codified in the form of a mark scheme.

Informal assessment was mentioned in the last section in the context of challenge. There we looked at how questions give us access to information about student learning, which we can then use to help them make great progress.

Here, we will focus on formal assessment.

When constructing a formal assessment for students to take – whether this is in the form of a test, or a task which asks them to create a certain piece of work such as an essay – you can use the taxonomy to frame your endeavours.

Any assessment you construct will have as its aim the elicitation of information regarding student knowledge and understanding. An effective assessment will give students the opportunity to demonstrate the extent of what they know and what they can do. A circumscribed assessment is sometimes necessary to check recall or comprehension but, in general, we want to create opportunities through which understanding can be fully, and therefore accurately, gauged.

To this end, Bloom's Taxonomy can be employed. We can construct tests which ask students a series of questions about a particular topic, with these questions becoming increasingly demanding as they move up the taxonomy. Many formal assessments provided by exam boards are designed in precisely this way.

Earlier questions test knowledge and comprehension while later ones gradually move up the levels, often combining two or more assessment objectives at the same time.

When it comes to designing tasks which ask students to create products you will mark and assess, the same points hold. First, we want to give students the opportunity to showcase their knowledge and understanding – we want to avoid too much circumscription because this limits the extent of the information we are able to elicit, diminishing the efficacy of any judgements we subsequently make.

Two highly effective applications of the taxonomy suggest themselves (and to this whole topic we will return in more detail in Chapter Nine). First, we can create a series of sub-tasks within a main activity, with each of these based on sequential levels of the taxonomy (or various combinations thereof). Such activities are challenging at the same time as they give students the scope in which to demonstrate the extent of their knowledge and the depth of their understanding.

Second, we can give students a selection of success criteria based on the taxonomy. These will guide them, directing their work where we want it to go. Some students will be able to fulfil all the criteria, others won't. Either way, we will be in a position to accurately gauge where they are currently at. This is because the success criteria will have set a wide scope for the task, letting us elicit the most information possible about what students know and don't know as well as what they can and can't do.

This again demonstrates why the taxonomy works, and why it is such an effective tool on which all teachers can call during the course of their planning, teaching and marking. Its inherently progressive nature – the fact that it represents the constituents of mastery learning and, in so doing, sets out a framework of increasing cognitive complexity – means we can always use it to contrive challenging assessments which make a range of demands on student knowledge and understanding. This elicits the information we need to accurately judge the extent of students' learning as well as their relative proficiency in using this learning.

So there we have it. We have built on the initial analysis conducted in Chapter One, demonstrating how the taxonomy reflects the nature of thought and examining how it provides a simplified, practical model on which we can call time and again through the course of our work with students, older and younger, in relation to all different areas of the curriculum. Throughout this process we have further explained why the taxonomy works and, as a result, provided a strong rationale for its continued and frequent application inside and outside the classroom.

With our groundwork complete, let us now turn to matters practical. First, we will divide the taxonomy into three pairings and look at how we can make best use of these. Then, we will look at a series of different lesson elements, examining how we can best apply the taxonomy in each case.

Chapter Three – Knowledge and Comprehension

Outline

In this chapter we will consider knowledge and comprehension, the first two levels of the taxonomy, in the context of the classroom. To begin, we will examine each category, drawing out practical examples of its application to teaching and learning. We will then look at knowledge and comprehension as the basis for learning in any given lesson, before going on to look at their use in starter activities, the first sections of lessons and at the beginning of main activities.

As a reminder, here are the knowledge and comprehension keywords from Chapter Two:

Knowledge:

Arrange, Define, Describe, List, Match, Memorise, Name, Order, Quote, Recognise, Recall, Repeat, Reproduce, Restate, Retain.

Comprehension:

Characterise, Classify, Complete, Describe, Discuss, Establish, Explain, Express, Identify, Illustrate, Recognise, Report, Relate, Sort, Translate.

Knowledge in Detail

Knowledge means being able to recall pieces of information. This information is usually in the form of words. Those words may be recalled verbally or in writing. Without knowledge of the words connected to a topic, as well as words more generally, it will be difficult, sometimes impossible, for students to think further about the matter in question. This is because they will struggle to articulate themselves, having no linguistic means to do so. Articulation could come through other means – gesture and image for example – but this will be necessarily less precise and, being a different form to that of language, have less scope and relevance in the classroom.

(As an aside, remember that we are concentrating on the cognitive domain. Knowledge can also mean knowing how to do things, and this knowing is not necessarily so bound up with words. However, much of this which is relevant to the classroom – such as in Art, Drama, DT and PE – is beyond the scope of this book, dealing as it does with the psychomotor domain).

To begin the study of any topic then, students need to know things.

This means knowledge is always the starting point of individual lessons and schemes of work. However, this starting point has two sides to it. First, we have the knowledge students need to possess to be able to engage with the topic and make progress. Second, we have the knowledge students already possess and which relates to the topic in question.

When we begin planning a lesson, we must think about both these things.

Similarly, whenever we start teaching a new topic, we should always try to ascertain the extent of students' prior knowledge. Here are five simple ways to do this:

- Ask students to list everything they know about the topic.

- Ask students to create a spider diagram about the topic.

- Ask a series of open questions through which students can articulate and discuss their existing knowledge.

- Ask students to work in pairs. Each member has one minute to explain everything they know about the topic. Meanwhile, the teacher circulates and listens.

- Ask students to predict what they think the lesson will cover, based on what they already know about the topic, and to explain or defend their predictions.

In each case, our aim is to elicit information about the knowledge students already possess. We can then teach and plan lessons which more accurately meet the needs of our students. For example, we might be teaching a Religious Studies lesson on the topic of Christian ethics. Finding out in advance or at the start of the lesson what students already know about Christianity, ethics and Christian ethics will help us to immediately begin building on existing knowledge, rather than rehashing old ground.

So knowledge as the starting block of all subsequent learning always has these two elements to it, both of which we must consider:

- What we think students need to know about a topic.

- What students already know about a topic (including related or tangential knowledge).

Highly effective teaching sees students making significant, sustained progress. This is easier to achieve if we have a clear sense of the knowledge students need to acquire about a given topic as well as the knowledge they already possess.

If we fail to take account of either one of these, our planning becomes less closely focused on the students in front of us and less concerned with accurately teaching the relevant curriculum area.

A useful means through which to track student knowledge is a subject knowledge audit. Here, we provide students with a breakdown of all the elements of the curriculum we intend to look at over a given period. Next to each element there are five columns, labelled with the numbers 1 to 5. 1 means no or little knowledge. 5 means excellent, detailed knowledge.

At the start of the topic, students take a coloured pen and go through the audit, marking where they think they are at in relation to each piece of knowledge (by ticking the relevant column). They then return to this audit sheet during the course of the topic and use a different coloured pen to mark where their knowledge is now. You can repeat this process on a number of occasions. It shows students what they know, what they don't, and what progress they make. It also gives you access to all this information.

Comprehension in Detail

Comprehension refers to our ability to understand the knowledge we have acquired. Knowing something does not mean we understand. The history of love is proof positive of this fact – as poets and authors have told us for hundreds of years.

Turning to a prosaic example, consider the student who can recite a poem, having learnt it off-by-heart. We might ask them what the poem means only to find them staring blankly at us. They do not know what it means. They only know what the words are, the order in which they come and how they should be articulated.

Comprehension follows knowledge (it cannot come before because it is the knowledge we are comprehending). But it does not follow by necessity. Work needs to take place. Learning needs to happen.

As a result, we must be careful when assessing students' prior knowledge (as advocated in the previous section) that we do not mistake knowing for understanding. To ascertain the status of the knowledge students possess – whether it is simply recall of facts or whether it includes the ability to explain and illustrate those facts – we need to ask slightly more complex questions or set slightly more challenging tasks.

Here are five examples of how we might do this at the start of a lesson, with the intention of assessing the degree of understanding students possess:

- Ask students a series of comprehension-based questions such as 'Can you explain x?' or 'What would you say X means?' or 'Why might X be relevant to our topic?'

- Ask students to recall everything they know and then to select what they believe are the three most important pieces of information – and to provide justification for their choices.

- Ask students to work in pairs. One student should play dumb. The other student should explain what they understand about the topic. Meanwhile, the teacher circulates and listens.

- Ask students to make a list of what they know about the topic and then to come up with five questions they would like answered to help deepen their understanding.

- Ask students to interview each other to find out what they already know and understand about the topic. Provide sample questions as a model for students to imitate.

Compare these tasks to those outlined in the previous section on knowledge. You will immediately notice the difference in complexity. You will also see how the latter explicitly rest on the former – reinforcing the idea that comprehension can never come before knowledge, only after.

As with knowledge, if we have a clear sense of what students understand about the topic then we can plan and teach lessons which facilitate greater progress. We will avoid revisiting old ground and will not waste time trying to establish comprehension our learners already possess.

Knowledge as the Starting Point

Knowledge is a necessary and useful starting point for lessons. It gives students the foundations from which to make progress, providing the information they must acquire if they are to be successful. Here are five ways in which you can use knowledge as the starting point of your planning and teaching:

- At the start of a topic, identify all the knowledge you believe a student will need to possess by the end of the unit of work to be highly successful. Make a list of this and then work backwards, identifying where and when they will be able to gain access to this information. Here, we are defining the extent of the knowledge we expect students to acquire before planning the opportunities through which they can acquire this.

- When planning a single lesson, identify what knowledge you would like students to possess by the end. Think from the perspective of a successful student who makes excellent progress through the course of the lesson. Having identified the knowledge, work backwards to plan your lesson, ensuring each section provides students with the necessary opportunities to acquire what you have identified. This is a development of the first point, based on one lesson rather than a series.

- At the start of a unit of work, provide students with a guidance sheet indicating all the knowledge you expect them to acquire by the end. Talk them through this sheet at the beginning of the first lesson and refer back to it in subsequent lessons, giving them the opportunity to tick off what they have learned. This gives students a sense of ownership over their learning by providing the framework of knowledge they need to acquire.

- When planning a unit of work, start with the assessment. Ask yourself what knowledge students will need to achieve full marks (as well as how they will need to manipulate this). Then, keep the assessment in mind while you plan. It will be the beacon at which you are aiming, ensuring your lessons cover everything students need to know to be successful.

- At the start of a lesson, ask students to review their learning from last time. They should identify the knowledge they acquired as well as any prior knowledge they used as part of their learning. Encourage them to discuss these points with a partner. The verbal articulation will help refine and reinforce their understanding of what they know. Having done this, introduce any new knowledge relevant to the present lesson. This will be immediately situated within students' prior learning (about which they have just been talking), helping them to quickly make sense of the new information.

Each of these examples illustrates how attending to knowledge allows you to clearly define and then build upon the foundations of learning in relation to a given topic. It also indicates how getting a clear sense of the knowledge students need to acquire can provide you with a guiding framework – one which helps you to plan well and to ensure nothing of importance is overlooked. In one sense, this process is about you synthesising the information set out in the curriculum so you can present it to students in the most effective way possible.

Comprehension as the Starting Point

An alternative starting point for your lessons is comprehension. This is inherently bound up with knowledge. When we look to it as a starting point, we do so while being aware that it rests on knowledge and is, put simply, the development of understanding in relation to this. Here are five ways you can use comprehension as the starting point of your planning and teaching:

- When planning an individual lesson, consider what you want students to understand at each stage of it. From here, you can develop activities which allow for the development of this understanding. You might choose to think about the ideal understanding you would like all students to develop, or you might opt for a graduated understanding reflecting the various starting points of all the students in your class.

- Ask yourself what question, or questions, you would like students to be able to answer come the end of an individual lesson or series of lessons. To do this, they will need to develop a certain level of understanding about the topic. You can work backwards from here, planning activities and tasks which facilitate such a development.

- Assess the quality of understanding students have about a topic. Then, ask yourself how far you would like this understanding to develop. For example, would you like it to be deeper, broader, more nuanced or, perhaps, all three. Having defined your aim you can set about planning lessons which will help you to achieve this.

- You may decide in a given case that for students to make the best progress possible they will need to be able to explain their understanding of certain relevant pieces of knowledge at the very start of the lesson. From here you can plan an opening activity which allows them to do just this. Or, as the case may be, gives you the opportunity to convey understanding to students, perhaps by modelling a thought process or explanation for them, which they go on to imitate and apply themselves.

- Identify in advance of your lesson what understanding you want students to develop. With this in mind, formulate two or three questions you can use to examine whether they have achieved this. One example are hinge questions. These allow you to test students' understanding about common misconceptions associated with the topic of study. The purpose here is to work out in advance how you will effectively judge the quality of understanding your students develop.

In these examples we see how thinking about comprehension allows us to build on the identification of relevant knowledge. Understanding becomes something defined and assessable. In our assessments we gain access to information which tells us how much progress students have made. We can use this to adapt our teaching, making it better in the process.

As with the points made regarding knowledge, we are doing a degree of synthesis throughout all of this. That is, we are working out in advance what we would like to see, given the material we know we are teaching. This places us in a strong position from which to teach, plan and assess effectively.

Using Knowledge and Comprehension as Lesson Starters

Knowledge and comprehension both make an excellent basis for lesson starters. This is for two reasons. First, starter activities predicated on these categories allow you to access, at the very beginning of your lesson, the existing knowledge and understanding your students possess. You can then use this information to inform your teaching. Second, activities based on these categories are relatively straightforward, meaning students can achieve them and experience success from the get go. This binds them into your lessons, raising motivation and engagement.

Here are ten starter activities, four based on knowledge, four based on comprehension and two based on a combination:

- Present students with the topic of study. Challenge them to list everything they already know about this. They should work individually at first, for sixty seconds. When the sixty seconds are up, invite students to get into pairs or threes and to compare their lists, seeing what is similar and what is different. **(Knowledge)**

- Present students with a range of keywords from a previous lesson. Challenge them to recall the definitions of these words. These can either be written down or discussed with a partner. **(Knowledge)**

- Ask students to work in pairs and to write the letters A-Z on a sheet of paper. Introduce the lesson topic and challenge the class to identify something connected to the lesson topic for each letter of the alphabet. The first pair to fill their sheet are the winners. **(Knowledge)**

- Present students with an image and ask them to discuss with their partner how it connects to the previous lesson or to the current lesson topic. Encourage students to make as many connections as possible by recalling everything they know about the previous lesson or current topic. **(Knowledge)**

- Present students with a piece of stimulus material related to the topic such as an image, a video clip, a piece of music or a source. Give them time to examine the stimulus material and to think about what it is and how it connects to the lesson. Next, reveal a series of questions about the material through which students have to show and/or develop their understanding of it. Questions can be answered individually or in pairs. **(Comprehension)**

- Mid-way through a topic, begin the lesson with three big questions connected to what you have already studied. Divide the class into three and assign one question to each third. Indicate students must be able to explain an answer to their question when called upon and that the rest of the class will judge whether their answer is right and whether anything could be added to it. Provide discussion time in advance of calling on students to answer. **(Comprehension)**

- Present students with a series of images connected to the topic you have been studying and ask them to explain what each image means or how it relates to the topic. You can extend this into application by challenging students to pick three different images which could have been used instead and to explain their choices. **(Comprehension)**

- Present students with a question along with four possible answers. Ask them to identify which is the right answer and to explain why it is right. This activity can be developed to include a series of questions, each with various answers. You can also ask students to work in pairs so that, on each occasion, they have to discuss their understanding. **(Comprehension)**

- Ask students to draw a spider diagram showing everything they know about the topic of study. When they have finished, ask them to explain how the information could be divided into two or three separate groups. You might want to suggest the groups yourself, or you might leave this for students to decide. **(Knowledge and Comprehension)**

- Present students with a set of keywords and a set of related images. The keywords and images should be jumbled up. Challenge students to match the keywords and images, explain the connections and give a definition for each keyword. **(Knowledge and Comprehension)**

These starters can be used across the curriculum, simply adapt them to fit the content you are teaching. You can also use them with different age-groups. Here, your adaptations will need to take account of the relative skills and abilities of your students. So, for example, the final starter is appropriate for seven year-olds and eighteen year-olds, but how you structure it, the keywords and images you choose, and the expectations you have for the depth of the explanations and the quality of students' definitions will vary in each case.

Using Knowledge and Comprehension in the First Half of Lessons

Knowledge and comprehension are also well-suited to being used in the first half of lessons. This is because they provide a framework on top of which more complex tasks can be placed – those involving the other four levels of the taxonomy. Also, if we see the lesson as a general upwards climb towards mastery, then the beginning will always have to contain at least some element of knowledge and comprehension, except for the situation where this has been done in the previous lesson (but even so, we still have the split wherein knowledge and comprehension come first).

Here, then, are five examples of how this plays out in practice.

- We decide to divide our lesson in two. In part one, we introduce students to the content, help them to memorise it and become familiar with it, then give them an activity or two through which they can develop their understanding of it. In the second half of the lesson we turn to application and analysis. Students have to solve a series of problems based on what they learned in the first half of the lesson. This classic structure perfectly demonstrates how knowledge and comprehension can act as the building blocks for deeper thought.

- Another common approach is to present students with a range of content and give them the first half of the lesson to work through this. For example, in a History lesson we give students a selection of sources and ask them to read through and make notes on these, with their notes structured in accordance with a set of questions (such as: Who? What? When? Where? Why?). In the second half of the lesson, we ask students to start interpreting the sources by looking at how they relate to each other. As part of this, we ask them to assess the relative reliability of the various sources. Again, we see the benefits which accrue when we start with knowledge and comprehension and then build up from there.

- If you prefer a higher degree of structure you might divide your lesson into three and assign each pairing of taxonomy levels to each section. You would start with knowledge and comprehension, then move to application and analysis before, in the final part of the lesson, asking students to synthesise and/or evaluate the material about which they have been learning. This approach sees mastery condensed into a single lesson. It relies on us laying down foundations before moving onto higher order thinking skills.

- Another option is to begin the lesson with a demonstration or some modelling. Students copy this and, through the first half of the lesson, the teacher uses questions to check and develop their understanding. For example, we might show students how to draw perspective, ask them to imitate our model, circulate and ask questions, and then lead a discussion examining why and how drawing in this way works. In the second half of the lesson we would invite students to apply their knowledge and understanding by creating their own images containing perspective (here, application, analysis and synthesis are rolled into one).

- Finally, we could begin the lesson with a knowledge-based starter activity like one of those outlined above before moving into an exploratory discussion concerning the topic of study and all those things connected to it. The point of this discussion would be to broaden and deepen students' understanding of the lesson content. In the second half, we might challenge students to produce a speech putting forward their views on the content. This would draw on the comprehension they developed during the discussion (with some analysis and application perhaps present as well).

In each of these examples we see how starting with knowledge and comprehension puts students on the path to mastery. The aim is to build a firm foundation which forms the basis of effective, challenging higher order thinking.

It should also be noted that in the examples we once more see how the levels of the taxonomy interlink. While knowledge and comprehension are advocated as starting points for many lessons, they will not always be the *exclusive* focus of the first half the lesson; often, in fact, they will be the *primary* focus, with some of the other levels creeping into view as well.   .

Using Knowledge and Comprehension at the Start of Activities

Our final section looks at a slightly different approach: constructing multi-part activities in which knowledge and comprehension form the start; the first rung on the ladder, as it were. Here are three illustrative examples:

- Watch the video clip showing the experiment then answer the questions about what happened and what caused it. Next, try to work out what might happen if the experiment took place under different conditions. Think about the potential impact of changes in temperature, the presence of a catalyst, and if there was a different ratio of elements in the compound. Finally, assess what the experiment reveals to us about the nature of the compound as well as what it doesn't reveal. If possible, suggest how we could gain access to more information about the nature of the compound.

- Discuss the definitions with your partner. Do they make sense? Can you explain how you would use the words in a sentence? When you are happy that you understand the meanings of the words, go online and identify two recent news stories to which we could apply some of the terms. For example, you might find a story about police attitudes towards young people and then apply 'labelling' to it. Finally, assess whether or not all of the words are equally useful. Ask yourself what makes a concept useful to a sociologist and to what extent each of these words meets your criteria.

- Watch me as I show you how to strike the ball correctly. Get into pairs and practice copying what I've shown you. After that we'll get back together and discuss why this is the best way to strike the ball. Then, we're going to have a go at a pass and shoot activity where I want you to try to apply the technique at speed. Finally, we'll go into a series of 3 vs 3 games and I want you to focus on identifying when you should strike the ball in this way and when you should pass up the opportunity. You'll have to assess your options and play the percentages as effectively as possible.

In each of these examples we have a series of sub-tasks bound together in a single activity. They could be viewed as lessons in miniature, or you could have a lesson which contained two or three of these types of activities. You'll notice in each case we begin with knowledge and comprehension before moving up the taxonomy. As with the previous section, the aim is to quickly build a base of knowledge and understanding which students can then call on to learn more and make great progress. Another example of mastery learning in action.

That concludes our examination of knowledge and comprehension. We will come back to the categories, as we will come back to all six, in Chapters 6 – 10. For the moment, however, let us move on to examine application and analysis in (relative) isolation.

Chapter Four – Application and Analysis

Outline

In this chapter, our focus turns to application and analysis. We will first consider what each means in a practical context and how they can shape the learning we ask students to do. Then, we will examine how each process can be a point of development within a given lesson, following initial steps centred on knowledge, comprehension or both. Next, we will look at how we can use application and analysis as the basis for activities before going on to see how targeted application can help to accelerate learning and why analysis is central if we want to promote deeper understanding.

My aim is to provide clear guidance on how you can use application and analysis and to give a range of practical examples you can apply, adapt or develop in the context of your own teaching.

As a reminder, here are the application and analysis keywords from Chapter Two:

Application:

Apply, Calculate, Choose, Demonstrate, Dramatize, Employ, Implement, Interpret, Operate, Perform, Practise, Role-Play, Sketch, Solve, Suggest.

Analysis:

Analyse, Appraise, Categorize, Compare, Contrast, Differentiate, Discriminate, Distinguish, Examine, Experiment, Explore, Investigate, Question, Research, Test.

Application in Detail

We apply knowledge and understanding. That is, we take what we know and what we understand and we use it in situations other than that with which we are familiar. So, for example, we apply our knowledge to solve a problem or we use our understanding to overcome an obstacle.

If we attend to what we are doing during the process of application then we come to further develop the knowledge and understanding we seek to apply. This is because the information and experience to which the application (or attempted application) gives rise is a supplement to our present knowledge and understanding of the thing in question.

For example, we might know and understand what the water cycle is. Then, we might find ourselves faced with the challenge of applying this knowledge and understanding to a situation in which one part of the cycle appears to be out of kilter. As part of this application, we would be expected to ascertain why the cycle is not as we would expect it (and here, we can note how application and analysis are often intertwined).

During this cognitive process, we find ourselves taking what we already know and applying it to a new situation. Through this process we broaden and deepen our understanding and knowledge. The expression of what we know and think in the new context is, in itself, new information. A supplement to what we already possess. In addition, the application causes us to look at our existing knowledge and understanding in a new light – to use it. This usage reveals further information about its nature and the extent to which it can be applied in a given situation.

For these reasons, application is always to be welcomed but active or targeted application – that is, application in which the student is consciously directing their effort in pursuit of a goal – is generally preferred. This type of application leads to greater learning gains than passive or undirected application.

A simple way in which to target application is to provide students with a structure – such as a set of success criteria or a checklist. Another option is to set targets and ask students to implement these while they apply their knowledge and understanding.

If we take a step back, away from the classroom, and think about learning more generally, we can see just how important application is to the pursuit of mastery. This point is encapsulated in the familiar adage, 'practice makes perfect.' Indeed it does. But attentive practice makes perfect more quickly. This is because the attention we direct affords us the opportunity to learn continuously from the process of application, furthering the development of our knowledge and understanding more swiftly than would otherwise be the case.

During lessons, providing opportunities for students to apply their learning means giving them a chance to take the basics and then broaden and deepen this. In a sense, the process is about widening the experience students have of whatever content the lesson concerns.

Returning to the idea of problem-solving, we can see how a student who is given the chance to apply their knowledge and understanding to a series of different problems will, on each occasion, gain experience of the scope, nature and applicability of that knowledge. It is for this reason that there is a strong connection between expertise and repeated practice. Without sufficient opportunity to apply that which we have memorised and come to understand, we lose the chance to know and understand it in the wider context.

To reiterate, applying knowledge and understanding gives rise to at least two important opportunities, from both of which learning stems.

First, we gain access to information about the efficacy of applying what we know and understand in a given situation. We broaden and deepen what we already have. Second, the application is itself new knowledge – a supplement, enhancing the position from which we began.

A final example helps to reinforce the point.

Consider a trainee glass-blower who has a basic knowledge and understanding of the trade in which she is apprenticed. Take her out of the learning process at this point and her stock of learning is limited. Allow her to apply what she has by trying to blow glass in the workshop and, on every occasion that she engages in application, she learns. That learning encompasses the effects of her efforts as well as the process of applying her efforts. Both give access to new learning. Both help her to become more proficient and more skilled in applying the knowledge and understanding in new contexts.

Analysis in Detail

Analysis is closely connected to application. If we actively attend to the results of any application of knowledge and understanding we make, then we are, at least in part, analysing the results of our endeavours. This analysis involves examining what we are doing and noting its effects, as well as considering how our actions relate to other aspects such as the finished products which result. Furthermore, in looking at the similarities and differences between our expectations of what application will bring and the actual results of our application, we are once again engaging in analysis.

For example, I might apply my knowledge and understanding of cooking fish to a new problem: how to cook river cobbler, a fish I have not cooked before. I examine the fish and note it's similarity to other types of white fish with which I am familiar. As a result, I decide to apply my existing knowledge and understanding by wrapping the fish in lightly oiled foil and placing a piece of lemon inside the resulting parcel. I place the fish in the oven and, after ten minutes or so, take it out.

Next I open up the foil parcel and begin to examine the fish. I compare the results to my knowledge and understanding of what other white fish look like when cooked. I taste a piece and make further comparisons. Then I start to consider whether I should have seasoned the fish, what impact this might have had and whether or not I have cooked it for too long, in terms of the texture to which this has given rise.

This whole process is one on analysis. Analysis in which I am concerned with the results of my application. We can therefore see how use of the latter is frequently followed – or tied up with – use of the former. (Evaluation can come in here as well, such as when we assess the quality of our application or the extent to which the results match our expectations. This demonstrates that there is a fine line between analysis predicated on comparison and the act of judgement – which is, one might argue, a special case of comparison.)

We can also use analysis independently of application, however, or as a next step following success in the precursor.

So, for example, we might ask students to analyse a text with which they are unfamiliar. To do this, they will call on the prior knowledge and understanding they possess, with this having being previously developed through repeated application. This could see them analysing the effect a poem has on a reader, having previously learnt about some of the different tools literary critics can call on when dissecting a text and having then practised applying these to some simpler poems.

Here we see how the ability to effectively analyse does tend to rest on us having previously had the opportunity to work through the application of knowledge and understanding. Leaping straight from comprehension to analysis can be tricky as the extent of our comprehension may be limited by our inexperience in using it.

This is one of the reasons why we often, and often unconsciously, draw application and analysis together in the same activity. Whether explicitly stated or not, we understand that being able to do the latter well means having at least some practice in the former.

In some cases, of course, the analysis we ask students to do is of a more general type. In these situations, the jump between comprehension and analysis is not so great. This is because students have already learned how to apply certain skills or knowledge in general, and can now call on these in the context of new and specific knowledge or understanding. This is an example of what the oft-misused phrase 'transferable skills' means.

Because analysis is concerned with unpicking the nature of things, it gives access to further information and learning, helping us to progress further than if we stop at the level of application.

For example, I might master the art of applying gloss paint to the walls of my living room so it leaves a neat finish. But if I then began to analyse why this was the case, and to compare the use of gloss paint with other types of paint, my understanding would surely deepen.

I use this example quite specifically because it also illustrates why many students often feel it is OK to stop once effective application has been achieved. In the case of my living room walls, the questions which jump out at us are: Do you really need to engage in the analysis? Haven't you achieved what you wanted? Isn't going any further just doing it for the sake of it?

I'm sure you will have encountered students who convey these feelings in class. Once they can do the bare minimum to get by they are happy. Often, they then fail to accept, at first glance, the legitimacy of being expected to push on into the realms of analysis (and beyond).

Two points follow.

The first is that, if our aim is mastery, then application is not a sufficient endpoint. Mastering how to apply what we know and understand is not the same as mastering that content in full. What is more, by working our way through the levels of analysis, synthesis and evaluation, we come to see that what we previously perceived as the limits of our application were in fact only the limits that we could see at that point in time. Enhancing our understanding as we move up the taxonomy affords us the chance to look at our previous application in a new light; and to see that it was only ever partial.

Second, effective application includes being able to apply our knowledge and understanding in situations where we don't know what we are supposed to do. This is much easier to achieve if you have a degree of analytical and evaluative understanding, as well as some experience of using what you know to create or develop something new.

To put this another way, a critical and creative understanding of ideas and/or information and/or skills allows us to respond to uncertainty with greater confidence and effectiveness. Compare this to stopping at application. How do we know that the application we have mastered represents the extent of all the application there is? Answer: we don't.

I draw your attention to these points here both to stress the importance of analysis and to give you some useful tools through which to unpick and challenge any arguments students might make about why they feel it is unnecessary to challenge themselves beyond a certain level.

Having explored application and analysis in detail, let us now look at some specific manifestations in terms of teaching and learning.

Application as the Development Point

If we begin a lesson by focussing on knowledge and comprehension, we can move onto application as the development point. That is, the point from which we push students' thinking, helping them to learn more by challenging them to use the knowledge and understanding they have developed. Here are five examples of how we might do this:

- Set students a series of problems they have to solve, using the knowledge and understanding they have developed. This is perhaps the most familiar use of application as a development point. Problem-solving involves looking for answers or solutions. To do this, students need to apply what they know and understand and examine the results. Here we see our familiar friend trial and error coming back into the learning process, as well as more evidence of the relationship between application and analysis.

- Ask students to create a product based on their knowledge and understanding. For example, we might request a guide aimed at people who have never encountered our lesson topic before. This sees students applying what they know but doing so through the lens of writing for a particular audience.

- Challenge students to convey their understanding of the content through one or more forms. For example, we might ask a Citizenship class to make a comic strip showing what they understand about human rights, or we might ask an English class to produce a role-play showing how two Shakespearean characters might behave if they were transplanted into the modern day.

- Give students a selection of new material and ask them to group this according to what they already know and understand. For example, we give students a card sort containing various factors which influence immigration and ask them to group these into push and pull factors.

- Challenge students to suggest how they or someone else could use what they know and understand in a given situation. Case studies are a useful tool for this. For example, in a Design and Technology lesson we might give students a case study concerning a particular product and ask them to suggest how the sustainability of this could be improved, based on their knowledge of sustainable design and manufacture.

Analysis as the Development Point

Analysis can also be the development point for learning in our lessons. As mentioned earlier, this can be standalone or it can be interwoven with another level of the taxonomy – often application but sometimes also synthesis or evaluation. Here are five examples of activities you can try yourself:

- Ask students to compare and contrast two or more things. This is an analysis activity with which you will be very familiar. It is perhaps the most widely used example. The process of comparison involves analysing the nature and structure of the items in question. This helps students to gain a deep understanding of what the items are like, as well as how they relate to one another. A useful tool is to provide students with a list of questions on which they can base their comparison. This is particularly helpful for less-able students who may struggle to develop their comparisons in any depth.

- Challenge students to test a hypothesis. Such activities are not restricted to Science lessons. For example, in a History lesson we might ask students to test the hypothesis that World War Two was cause by the Treaty of Versailles. In testing a hypothesis, students have to break down the elements of that hypothesis, examine them, collect the results of their testing together and then use this to see whether the hypothesis can be proven or not (which, arguably, involves a degree of evaluation).

- Give students a topic they have to research along with a suitable research question. This means students remain analytical in their approach – because they know that, ultimately, they have to answer a question, rather than just collate disparate pieces of information.

- Set students a provocative, controversial or critical discussion question they have to answer by re-examining content with which they are already familiar. For example, you might pose a counter-intuitive or counter-factual question which students have to work in pairs to answer. To do this, they will have to go back over the learning they have done in the lesson and look at it from the new perspective provoked by the question.

- Challenge students to go over their work and analyse how it could be improved. To do this, they will need to distinguish between what is right and what is wrong, what is perfect and what could be better, as well as what is in need of refinement and what is already sufficiently refined. Here again we see the interweaving of analysis, application and evaluation in the same task, albeit with our main focus on the former.

Using Application and Analysis as the Basis for Activities

We move now to think a little more deeply about how application and analysis can form the basis of activities. This suggestion has been implicit above, where I have outlined ten examples of it in action. Here, I would just like to make a few points about the techniques and strategies you can employ to garner excellent results.

1. Ensure students are in possession of sufficient knowledge and understanding to gain significant benefits from your application and analysis activities. If their knowledge and understanding of the content is limited, then it will be harder for them to successfully apply this and to engage in analysis which is either critical or meaningful. Of course, if you feel your students will struggle to further develop their knowledge and understanding then you can simplify your application and analysis activities (essentially taking the reverse approach from that first suggested).

2. Use scaffolding and modelling to help students quickly and successfully access your activities. Scaffolding gives students a route into the successful completion of activities. It takes them some of the way, setting them on the path to success. We have given a couple of examples of this above where we suggested the provision of guidance questions or checklists on which students can call to complete an activity. Modelling

gives students a different insight, affording them a chance to witness what it is you would like them to do. They can then copy this, before internalising it and making it their own. Remember that modelling also includes the modelling of thinking.

3. Do not be frightened to plan opportunities for repeated application. Students may well need to practise applying knowledge and understanding multiple times before they fully master the process. This takes us back to that adage about practice making perfect...

You can vary things by giving students a range of different application procedures in which to engage and by throwing in caveats or additional challenges. The latter option is particularly good for challenging more-able students as they work through a series of application activities.

4. Be prepared to differentiate by planning application and analysis activities in tandem. Here, we set the class two activities to be done sequentially: first the application, then the analysis. But, we do so with the proviso that moving on should only happen once mastery of application has been achieved. Some students will move on and complete the analysis activity, some will move on but not finish it and some will remain working on the application task throughout. This is a good way to differentiate for a whole class while maintaining a high level of challenge for all.

Using Targeted Application to Accelerate Learning

Let us now turn to a point I made earlier about how targeted application can accelerate learning. This boiled down to a simple premise: if we direct our efforts and pay attention to the results then application of existing knowledge and understanding yields significant insights, speeding up learning.

Here are three examples of what this looks like in practice:

- Prior to the start of an application task, take a few minutes to carefully explain and model the success criteria to students. Invite students to talk to a partner about why these success criteria are relevant and what impact working towards them might have, in terms of learning. Start the activity and circulate through the room. Your focus should be exclusively on whether or not students are targeting their efforts in the direction of the success criteria. If they are not, draw their attention back to these and encourage them to refocus their efforts. At the end of the activity, lead students in a brief reflection in which you and they think about how knowledge and understanding have been enhanced by following the success criteria.

- Set up an activity in which students will be doing the same act of application three or four times, but with the emphasis each time on trying to work better than on the previous occasion. A good example is speed debating.

We split the class in two, present a statement and indicate that half the class will argue in favour and half will argue against. Students have ten minutes to develop their arguments. When the time is up, students pair up with somebody from the other half of the class. In each pair there is a member from each team. The teacher indicates which team will go first. These students have ninety seconds to put their arguments to their partner. When the time is up, the teams swap over. After that, there is a sixty second period in which both teams can speak, allowing students to argue concurrently in their pairs.

Next, the teacher asks one team to stand up and for all these students to find new partners. The activity then repeats. This whole process can be done two, three or four times. On each occasion, decrease the time available but indicate that students should still aim to convey the same amount of information to the same standard. The repeated application serves to help embed the ideas in students' minds as well as refine and develop these in light of the information they elicit through the process.

- Set up a series of stations around the room. Each one should contain a different problem connected to the topic of study. Divide students into groups. There should be the same number of groups as there are stations. Explain that groups will need to move around the room, visiting each station in turn. Their aim is to apply their knowledge on each occasion in an attempt to solve the problem with which they are faced. Provide groups with sheets on which they can note down their solutions.

The problems you place at each station should be similar but also different. They will be similar in the sense that they will all connect to the same topic – that about which students have developed a certain degree of knowledge and understanding. But they will vary by being different and by asking students to apply their knowledge and understanding in different ways.

As you will see, in each of these activities students are asked to repeatedly apply their knowledge and understanding in a relatively short space of time and to do so in relation to some clear target or purpose. This helps to accelerate learning and sustain great progress.

Using Analysis to Promote and Deepen Understanding

For our final section on application and analysis we will look at the latter and think about how it can be used to promote and deepen understanding. It does this by encouraging students to develop a more critical perspective on that with which they are familiar. By more critical we mean that students come to see whatever is in question in shades of grey, rather than in black and white. This is because analysis reveals the structure of things, taking us below the surface and, in the process, challenging the assumptions we might have developed when we first encountered information or ideas.

Here are three examples of how you can use analysis to promote and deepen understanding:

- Pose critical, challenging questions to students. These can be verbal or written. They can form the basis of the lesson, of activities, of discussions, or of extension tasks. You can also ask students analytical questions while they are engaged in activities of other types. For example, you might walk around the room and pose critical questions to a series of students to challenge their current thinking on the topic.

- Give students a checklist of analytical questions they can use again and again to think critically about the subject you are teaching. Here we are modelling thinking for students, providing them with a framework for critical thought relevant to a particular area. For example, we might give students a set of questions through which they can analyse information they extract from the internet. The intention is that students ask these questions every time they find something they think might be of use. This helps them to consistently think more critically about the information they find than would otherwise be the case. You can develop suitable questions for a wide range of subjects. Students will need a visual reminder at first but should, over time, come to internalise the model you provide.

- Pursue a spirit of enquiry in your lessons. By this I mean that you turn the focus away from the transmission of knowledge and shine it instead on the pursuit of insight and understanding. This covers the transmission of knowledge, which we have already dealt with in the previous chapter, but also encourages the development of a critical, analytical mindset. You can promote such a spirit by posing your lesson objectives as questions, by using questions to frame the lessons and activities you plan, by regularly including testing, researching, investigating and experimenting in your lessons and by giving students opportunities to ask questions themselves – of you and the learning.

That concludes our initial examination of application and analysis. We will return to all the levels of the taxonomy as part of chapters 6 – 10. For now, let us move on to look at synthesis and evaluation.

Chapter Five – Synthesis and Evaluation

Outline

In this chapter we turn our attention to synthesis and evaluation, the top two levels of the taxonomy. We will begin by examining how these processes play out in a classroom context, looking at the impact they have on student learning and the kind of cognitive work they ask students to do. Then, we will examine how to use synthesis and evaluation as the end point of lessons. That is, the point the learning works towards. Following this, we will look at the two processes as a basis for challenge, considering how they can be used to structure activities and, finally, what role they can play in defining the products we ask students to create.

As a reminder, here are the synthesis and evaluation keywords from Chapter Two:

Synthesis:

Combine, Compose, Construct, Create, Devise, Design, Formulate, Hypothesise, Integrate, Merge, Organise, Plan, Propose, Synthesise, Unite.

Evaluation:

Appraise, Argue, Assess, Critique, Defend, Evaluate, Examine, Grade, Inspect, Judge, Justify, Rank, Rate, Review, Value.

Synthesis in Detail

Having acquired knowledge, come to understand that knowledge, learned how to apply it, analysed it and used it to support the process of analysing other things, we reach a point at which our proficiency concerning the information and/or ideas is reasonably good. We are well on the path to mastery. Or the first stages of mastery if nothing else.

By this point in our journey we have developed a fairly detailed, critical understanding of the material in question. This places us in a strong position from which to take what we know and build on it. To create; to develop.

One of the main reasons why synthesis comes so late in the taxonomy is because we cannot create something new until we have a sound understanding of what has come before. For example, I cannot provide an alternative to the use of fossil fuels if I do not first have a decent, reasonably detailed understanding of what fossil fuels are, how they work and how they are used.

Synthesis is not restricted to subjects traditionally associated with creativity, such as Art, Design, English Language and Drama. It permeates all areas of thought. Scientific progress is frequently creative. As is the evolution of football tactics. So are revisionist interpretations of historical events. And new policy formulations put forward by earnest politicians (though maybe they could be a bit more creative!).

We need to disabuse students of any notion they might have that creative endeavour is restricted to a certain section of the curriculum. Undoubtedly, synthesis may be more readily apparent in some areas than others – and may attract greater rewards – but that it is relevant throughout is unarguable.

Having gone through the considerable groundwork of knowledge, comprehension, application and analysis, we find ourselves in a position from where we can look back at what we know and consider what its limits and extents are, in so far as we can see them. Then, we can think about how to make changes. This is one example of synthesis in action.

Another is when we look at what we know and understand and begin to make connections which were previously difficult to see (because of the limitations inherent in our earlier, less masterful understanding). These connections may be within given areas of our understanding or they may be between separate areas. An example of the first case would be a student who suggests an alternative to fossil fuels would be to build new settlements which promoted the use of renewable energy because of their placement and design. An example of the second case would be a student who suggests that an alternative to fossil fuels could be found by examining the factors which speeded up innovation at the start of the Industrial Revolution and then applying these to our modern day context.

And a third way in which synthesis comes into play is through the gradual developments afforded by repeated, closely analysed trial and error. Here we find ourselves thinking back to the feedback loop we outlined earlier in the book, whereby minor or major changes lead to mistakes and failures, but these are seen as opportunities from which to learn, due to the information they generate. This information is taken and analysed, with the results of the analysis informing the next attempt at synthesis. Eventually, so it is hoped, though this is not always the case, these repeated trials and errors lead either to the end we sought when we set out on our mission, or to a different end which proves nonetheless fruitful in what it yields.

Synthesis is not restricted to these three manifestations. But each one does, in its own way, represent a significant portion of the type of synthesis we are likely to ask students to do in the classroom (or that they will engage in on their own initiative).

You will note that the three approaches I have outlined could be said to interweave. This is true. It could also be said that I have been too forceful in my suggestion of the differences between the approaches.

Addressing the first point, as with other cognitive processes spoken of in this book, interweaving is true and is an accurate term to describe the reality of our experience. However, and as has been the case elsewhere, the aim here is simply to provide a useful working model we can seek to apply. This is more easily achieved through delineation.

In terms of the second point, I do not think it helpful for the teacher to conceive as synthesis as a single whole. For me, this makes the use and promotion of the process more difficult than it needs to be. By having three fairly distinct models on which we can call, we find ourselves better equipped to plan lessons which fit closely to our purposes and to encourage students to think in ways we feel are most useful in the context of the topics we are teaching.

In summary, all synthesis aims at the same end: the creation of that which is new. To achieve this, the synthesiser needs a sound knowledge and understanding of what is already the case, ideally underpinned by critical analysis. Different approaches to synthesis can be used and these reflect the different intellectual endeavours undertaken in the name of creativity. That these approaches are similar is admitted, that they are identical is not. Finally, in terms of teaching it remains the case that rough yet practical models are nearly always preferable to perfect yet cumbersome theories. That is the case here. That is what I have tried to outline. That is what I will exemplify below.

Evaluation in Detail

We move now to evaluation, which can be thought of as the peak of the taxonomy, the equal of synthesis or the fifth level of sixth (with its creative counterpart beating it to the top). But that is old ground for us, ground we dealt with early on. So let us turn our attention to the nature of evaluation.

Here we are concerned with judgement and assessment, with the ability to rank, value and appraise. It is the first of these keywords, I would argue, which gives us the greatest insight into the nature of evaluation. Passing judgement means coming to some type of informed decision on a matter of importance. That importance might be personal, moral, or, as in the case of the much teaching and learning, made important due to the behest of someone else (in this case, the teacher or the government).

Of course, we often make decisions and pass judgement on inconsequential matters, yet I would venture to say that their very inconsequentiality serves to make them matters on which little of our intellectual capacities are exercised. This means the judgements we form are not particularly evaluative. Like the subjects to which they refer, they carry little depth.

In terms of teaching and learning, we would like our students to develop good judgement, sound judgement and the ability to make informed, critical judgements. Each of these descriptors indicates the extent to which evaluation applied in the context of the classroom has meaning.

That meaning derives from two facts. First, that it connects to the learning in which students engage, learning which is deemed important. Second, that it connects to the critical faculties of the students we teach, faculties it is inherently good to possess.

This brief diversion illustrates that judgement is a large sphere and that we are focussed on an area relevant in the context of learning. So we can jettison those less important matters of judgement such as whether to have tea or coffee at break-time.

When we ask students to make a judgement we ask them to take all that they know and understand regarding a topic and to apply this to help them weigh up the relative merits of some particular thing. These merits are considered in light of certain criteria – they must be, otherwise no judgement can be made. This is because they very act of judging always involves the invocation of something against which the judgement rests.

For example, if I ask a student to assess whether or not a story has a good ending, the quality of their judgement will rest in large part on their knowledge and understanding of what constitutes a good ending as well as their ability to call this into action for the purposes of a critical comparison.

Here we can see the proof of the maxim that wisdom tends to come from experience. This is because through experience we gain a wider, deeper, more nuanced set of criteria against which to make our judgements. Therefore, our judgements become better. (Although a problem is that our judgements might also become more stuck in the mud, with the weight of experience acting against the possibility of new developments. Classic examples of this are outlined in Thomas Kuhn's book, *The Structure of Scientific Revolutions*.)

Returning to the classroom, we can see that evaluation in itself is not tricky. We could all throw out a judgement at random about anything, whether we were familiar with it or not. What is difficult is making good judgements. That is, judgements which are supported by strong reasoning, evidence, examples and arguments of other types (such as analogy, though this is itself a type of reasoning).

Students understand this. Even those who pay the least attention to the workings of their minds recognise that the quality of judgements runs along a continuum from excellent to woeful.

When we set them an evaluation task they recognise it for what it is: challenging. Unfortunately, this can lead some students to disengage. Usually, it is because the level of challenge feels too high for them. They look at the judgement they are being asked to make and recoil because they either do not understand how to do it successfully or because they recognise that the knowledge and understanding on which they can call is not sufficient to complete the task.

This is an inevitable occurrence we all experience from time to time – though hopefully not too much!

Before we move on, I want to suggest three simple strategies you can employ to neutralise such situations and help students stretch their own thinking in the process.

First, we can model the process of evaluation for our students, walking them through the steps we would take when making the kind of judgement we have asked them to make. We might do this verbally to begin with before writing down the process and annotating it. Students can then apply our model to make their own judgements (note how we have taken them back down the taxonomy, allowing them to engage with the task at a less complex level so that, over time, they can come to meet it on their own terms).

Second, we can make the criteria of judgement explicit. If we go back to the example used above, regarding whether the ending of the story is good or not, we can make life easier for students by setting out what constitutes a good ending (in a series of short bullet points, say) and then asking them to use these criteria as the basis of their judgement. Again we are, in part, taking them back down the taxonomy – here inviting them to do both analysis and application of the criteria we give them. But this is still in relation to the process of evaluation, thus making a sort of proxy-evaluation, or scaffolding, which helps students to reach the higher level process in the medium- and long-term.

Third, we can work with the students who recoil from evaluation to ascertain what their current knowledge and understanding of the topic entails. This process of eliciting information helps us to understand where the gaps in their learning are, as well as whether or not they have struggled with earlier parts of the taxonomy (such as analysis and application). Here we are seeking to review the foundations our students possess, so as to work out whether these are sufficiently developed to make effective evaluation a genuine possibility. Having diagnosed any gaps, errors or areas of weakness, we can address these, giving students an improved knowledge and understanding they can use to reattempt their evaluation.

We turn now to a range of practical strategies, activities and techniques based around synthesis and evaluation.

Synthesis as the End Point

First up is the idea of using synthesis as the end point of your lessons. This means we are asking students to work towards a point at which they can create something new – or can use their knowledge and understanding to suggest new ideas, applications or ways forward. Reaching this position indicates a good degree of mastery has been achieved over the lesson content. Here are three examples of the approach in action:

- In a History lesson we may build up towards a final activity in which students have to develop their own interpretation of an event they have been learning about. The quality of this interpretation will rest in large part on the quality and depth of understanding students have been able to build during the previous activities. Developing an interpretation involves taking this understanding (predicated on knowledge and, hopefully, analytical in nature) and marshalling this to produce some kind of coherent overview.

- In a Science lesson looking at the functions of the digestive system we might move towards a final activity in which students have to plan their own investigations. To help them do this we would provide a list of possible areas around which their investigations might focus. Other than that, it would be for students to decide how to use their knowledge and understanding to create a potentially useful and relevant investigation.

- In an English lesson looking at the role of dialogue in stories we could build towards a final activity in which students have to create a dramatic role-play illustrating how different techniques can be employed to make dialogue effective. Here it is presupposed that the lesson has been built around understanding and analysing these techniques.

In each of these cases you can see how the lesson is planned with the end in mind. That end is a synthesis-based activity asking students to make creative use of their prior learning. Through doing this they gain a greater insight into what they have learned, pushing their understanding beyond its current extents and enabling them to see connections which might otherwise have remained hidden.

The examples demonstrate both how and why synthesis as the end point represents an ascent to mastery or, depending on how effective the prior learning has been, a movement towards greater mastery than would otherwise have been the case.

Evaluation as the End Point

We can also use evaluation as the end point of our lessons. The principle is exactly the same – we ensure an increasing level of challenge by working our way up the levels of the taxonomy so that, by the last activity, students are still having their thinking pushed as they come ever closer to mastering the content. Here are three examples of the approach in action:

- At the start of a Sociology lesson we present students with a statement connected to the topic. For example (when studying crime and deviance): 'All crime is the result of poverty.' Through the course of the lesson we refer back to this, using it to frame the learning. Then, for the last activity, we invite students to use everything they have learned about crime and its links to poverty to assess the extent to which they agree or disagree with the statement. Here, all the learning from the lesson is required to make an effective judgement. Not only does such an approach have the benefit of promoting mastery, but so too does it help students to see the progress they have made – because they can quickly and easily compare the thoughts they had about the statement at the start of the lesson to the informed judgement they are able to make at the end.

- During a Maths lesson we introduce students to three different procedures for solving the same type of problem. The lesson is divided into five. We have a short starter activity, followed by three episodic activities. In each of these we introduce students to a different procedure and give them an opportunity to apply and analyse it. Finally, in the fifth part of the lesson, we ask students to assess which of the methods they think is most effective and why. To help them, we draw their attention to some of the strengths and weaknesses of the various procedures, before leaving them to develop a nuanced judgement themselves, supported by reason, evidence and examples.

- At the end of a PE lesson we ask students to conduct a self-assessment in which they judge the extent to which they have effectively implemented the skill we taught them. To support students we provide a set of success criteria and invite them to discuss the process of self-assessment with a partner, helping them to verbalise their thoughts about what signifies an accurate and precise implementation of the skill in question.

Notice how, in each of these case, students are turning around and looking back at their learning, using it for a productive end (the passing of judgement). This indicates how evaluation is similar to synthesis, as well as how it represents a point of mastery (because it rests on the prior learning one has amassed).

Using Synthesis and Evaluation as the Basis of Challenge

Another, fairly obvious, use of synthesis and evaluation is as the basis of challenge within lessons. This can come in three different forms. First, in the manner outlined above, where students work towards a challenging end point; one in which they have to synthesise or evaluate the lesson content.

Second, is where we use evaluation and synthesis tasks or sub-tasks throughout the lesson. As you can imagine, this creates a really high level of challenge. To that end, it is best used later on in a unit of work, when students have already established a good working knowledge and understanding of the content.

Third, involves us setting extension tasks and questions for students, either as part of the main activity (such as when we connect together a series of sub-tasks) or as supplements to the main activity (the classic 'extension question' students complete when they have finished the main piece of work). These tasks and questions are open to all students. Anyone who gets all their work done can have a go at them and enjoy the challenge which results. However, there is also an understanding that they will tend to be used by more-able students. In this sense they are a classic and familiar differentiation technique.

We will look at using Bloom's Taxonomy to stretch and challenge students' thinking in more detail in Chapter Ten.

Using Synthesis and Evaluation to Structure Assessment

Synthesis and evaluation can be used to structure assessments in three specific ways:

1. Having identified the two processes as being indicative of mastery we can create assessments in which we work backwards from either one. For example, we might plan an end-of-unit assessment in which students have to create an evaluative summary of the topic as a whole. Or, we might ask students to create something which demonstrates the detailed understanding they have developed through the course of the previous lessons.

Whatever we choose, the process is the same. We identify which of the two categories we want to prioritise and construct a task giving students the opportunity to show what they can do. To provide students with a chance to pick up marks by employing lower levels of the taxonomy, we could include a series of success criteria or sub-tasks which build up towards the creation of the final product.

2. We can create assessments containing a series of questions gradually progressing up the taxonomy from comprehension to synthesis and evaluation. These two categories form the basis of the final questions and it is for these that the greatest rewards are available. This is because they are the hardest things we are asking students to do. This is the structure of assessment favoured by many exam boards.

3. We begin by identifying how to assess students' learning at the end of the topic – whether we will focus on evaluation, synthesis or a combination of the two. Then, we think about what students will need to know and understand to be successful, as well as how they should be able to apply and analyse the knowledge and understanding they come to possess.

Next, we divide up the points we identified and use these as the basis of the lessons we plan. This way, we can be sure that we are teaching towards the challenging assessment piece on which we first decided. Each lesson contributes to the stock of knowledge and understanding students need to establish if they are to perform effectively in the final assessment.

Using Synthesis and Evaluation to Create Products

To conclude our section on synthesis and evaluation – as well as this first half of the book – we will think about the idea of products in a bit more detail. We touched on this earlier when looking at synthesis and evaluation as the end points of our lessons.

Products are the things we want students to create. The act of creation is an act of synthesis, as we know. With that said, the products we plan for can have varying focuses. For example, we could plan a fairly simple product involving students mostly just applying the knowledge they have acquired. This might be fine for an early or middle part of a lesson, but would not be sufficiently challenging later on.

Two points suggest themselves.

First, when designing tasks or planning the products we want students to produce in order to achieve, demonstrate and reinforce mastery, we can always turn to the keywords outlined at the start of this chapter. Using these as the basis of our tasks or plans means we are immediately pushing student thinking down the paths of synthesis and/or evaluation. This is a simple means through which to ensure you ask for products which are challenging, intellectually demanding and high quality.

Second, if we find ourselves asking students to create products we feel are not challenging enough, or if we think there is ambiguity about precisely what it is we expect, then we can provide synthesis and/or evaluation based success criteria which take students in the direction we want them to go. To do this we need only return to the keywords outlined above.

And that really does bring this section of the book to a close. In the second half we will look through the lens of lesson elements, examining how we can use the taxonomy to promote outstanding teaching, planning, marking and learning in the context of objectives and outcomes, activities and products, questioning, assessment and stretch and challenge.

Naturally, we have touched on all these areas already. We have done so, however, while focussing on the taxonomy and its individual levels as our main subject. In what follows, we turn the focus around, revealing a wide range of strategies, activities and techniques on which we can call.

Chapter Six – Objectives and Outcomes

In this chapter we examine the ways in which Bloom's Taxonomy can be used to structure learning objectives and learning outcomes. These are sometimes referred to as lesson objectives and lesson outcomes. For our purposes we will use the first formulation while considering the two interchangeable.

My aim is to demonstrate a variety of practical applications of the taxonomy to lesson planning. This builds on the thinking we did in the preceding chapters. We begin by attending briefly to the nature and purpose of objectives and outcomes, as well as the differences between the two.

Learning Objectives and Outcomes – A Brief Overview

Objectives and outcomes underpin lessons. When planning, you may choose to begin by defining them or you may prefer to plan the lesson first and then codify them. Either approach is reasonable. In the first case, the objectives and outcomes provide a starting point from which to move off. In the second case, we have a loose idea of them in our minds but only fully define this when we have finished putting the lesson together.

Learning objectives are the things towards which our lessons work. They are the goal. This is what an objective is: something we want to achieve. By having an objective, we have something guiding our lesson and, as a result, the learning we seek to promote.

Learning outcomes are the things we want our students to be able to do by the end of the lesson. If they can do them, they will have achieved the objective. The extent to which they can do them will demonstrate the extent to which they have achieved the objective. This is why we usually have multiple outcomes, often defined as:

- All will be able to...

- Most will be able to...

- Some will be able to...

Here we see that outcomes take account of the different rates of progress students in our class are likely to make. While we would prefer all students to fully achieve the learning objective, this is often unrealistic. Progress is about travelling forwards from a starting point, not about all students achieving exactly the same.

So we have objectives to give our lessons purpose and we have outcomes to define what achieving that purpose looks like, to greater or lesser extents. The first is the goal, the second are the ways in which the goal is met.

Sharing objectives and outcomes with students is seen as best practice. This is because doing so, it is argued, contributes to the useful notion of opening up success criteria. By doing this, we help students gain a clear understanding of what they need to do to be successful.

So, for example, we might explain the learning objective to students at the start of the lesson, refer to this in a mid-lesson review and then again in the plenary, giving students the chance to assess, on each occasion, how close they are to achieving it.

Similarly, we might show students what outcomes we expect them to achieve by the end of the lesson. This could be in the form of a written description displayed on the board, or through a piece of exemplar work used as a model.

In both these examples, we are giving students access to information which makes it easier for them to understand what success ought to entail. By opening up the criteria internal to the lesson, we give students a better chance of meeting or surpassing those criteria.

Alternative approaches do exist, however.

The first of these is to turn objectives and outcomes into a series of questions, as opposed to a series of statements. Doing this makes the content more accessible and promotes a general sense of enquiry. There is an emphasis on the idea that the purpose of the lesson is to reach a point where the various questions can be answered successfully, which is tangibly different from working towards being able to match or surpass a set of statements.

Another option is to construct objectives and outcomes in negotiation with students. The benefit here is that students can feel more engaged in the lesson and, as a result, more motivated to pursue the path to mastery which you as the teacher advocate. Two potential problems are that students may struggle to articulate suitable objectives/outcomes and that those they do suggest do not accord with your wider aims. Here it is worth returning to the opening sentence, where we used the word 'negotiation.' Thinking about the process in this way helps remind us that neither problem is insurmountable.

Overall, objectives and outcomes give structure to our lessons, purpose to our endeavours and concrete reference points against which to judge the learning students do. While we can formulate them in multiple ways, these points remain central in all cases. With these basic arguments established, we can now look at how to apply the taxonomy.

Creating Challenging Objectives

Maximising progress is one of the central goals of teaching. It encompasses raising achievement and giving students the best possible opportunity to learn and develop. If we set learning objectives which are too easy or too simple, achieving this end becomes difficult. Students faced with low expectations know, whether consciously or not, that what they need to do to be successful is not particularly demanding.

With too easy objectives, there is little or no chance of students rising to a challenge and making better progress than they believed themselves capable of.

This means that, if we want to teach as well as possible, we need to set challenging learning objectives at all times. That is, objectives which require effort, application and careful thinking if they are to be achieved.

The taxonomy clearly lends itself to such an aim. In most situations, we can call on the top three levels – analysis, synthesis and evaluation – to develop suitably challenging objectives. The process is simple. Return to the keywords first seen in Chapter Two, select one which fits with the lesson you are teaching and use it as the basis of your objective. Here are some examples:

LO: To assess the arguments for and against the use of proportional representation

LO: To create an alternative ending to the story of Little Red Riding Hood

LO: To investigate the most effective way of limiting coastal erosion

In each case we have a combination of content and process. The process is that defined by the keyword taken from the taxonomy while the content is that information on which the lesson focuses. We are using the keywords to create a statement describing what we want students to be able to do, cognitively, with the content about which we are concerned.

These exemplar objectives compare favourably to any we could construct using the lower levels of the taxonomy:

LO: To be able to recall the arguments for and against the use of proportional representation

LO: To understand the story of Little Red Riding Hood

LO: To show how coastal erosion could be limited by human intervention

Here we see the far lower level of challenge inherent in such objectives. What is more, what these objectives are asking students to do is in fact implicit within the original, more challenging set we provided. For example, we cannot assess the arguments for and against the use of proportional representation unless we can first recall them. Similarly, we cannot create a different ending for Little Red Riding Hood that works unless we first understand the story.

This takes us back to the earlier arguments concerning mastery and the fact that higher levels of the taxonomy rest on foundations predicated on the lower levels. Therefore, challenging objectives based on the top three levels will take care of the simpler cognitive processes at the same time as they push students to think more deeply about the lesson content.

We can also use the taxonomy keywords to create question-based learning objectives. Here are the three from above reworked accordingly:

LO: Are the arguments for proportional representation more persuasive than the ones against?

LO: How else could the story of Little Red Riding Hood turn out?

LO: Is it possible to effectively limit coastal erosion?

Immediately we see a significant difference. In these question-based formulations the keywords have disappeared. This reflects the nature and structure of questions, as well as the way in which we have tried to form these particular ones to make them engaging for students.

I flag up the point for one reason in particular. When getting used to applying the taxonomy for the purpose of creating question-style objectives, you might like to begin by developing statement-style objectives which you then turn into questions. This way, you can be sure your questions are closely tied to the level of the taxonomy towards which you are aiming.

This process has been exemplified above. First I came up with three learning objectives in statement form, using keywords from the taxonomy. Then I modified these so they were in the form of questions, with these closely mirroring the aims of the original objectives.

Finally, it is worth comparing the two sets of objectives:

LO: Are the arguments for proportional representation more persuasive than the ones against?

LO: To assess the arguments for and against the use of proportional representation

LO: How else might the story of Little Red Riding Hood turn out?

LO: To create an alternative ending to the story of Little Red Riding Hood

LO: Is it possible to effectively limit coastal erosion?

LO: To investigate the most effective way to limit coastal erosion

This comparison clearly demonstrates the differences between the two types of learning objective. They frame the lesson in different ways and make subtly different demands of students. They also imply different purposes, with the questions focussing more on enquiry than the statements.

All these points are worth considering when you decide what type of objectives to use in your planning.

Creating Differentiated Outcomes

Having defined our objective we now need to break this down into a series of outcomes. These are the things students will be able to do to show they have met the learning objective.

Differentiated outcomes take account of the different starting points possessed by our students, as well as the likelihood that not everybody will make the same degree of progress in any particular lesson.

The common formulation is All/Most/Some. This divides the class roughly into three groups, not necessarily of equal size. The 'all' outcome is the minimum everyone is expected to achieve. The 'more' outcome is that which most learners will access. While the 'some' target is generally reserved for the most able students.

One of the problems with differentiated outcomes is that they can set a ceiling on student achievement, labelling different groups as only capable of achieving certain outcomes. Three simple techniques help avoid this.

First, while continuing to use the all/most/some formulation, we make clear to students that this is for guidance only and that it does not refer to specific groups in the class. This implies the top levels of progress are open to everybody and, therefore, that nobody's efforts in pursuit of mastery will be wasted.

Second, we can get rid of the all/most/some nomenclature all together and replace it with something less strident in its delineation of difference. For example, some teachers like to use colours for different outcomes or, with younger students, related nouns such as types of fruit. Here, the aim is to maintain the difference between outcomes, as well as the sense of hierarchy in terms of increasing difficulty, but to communicate this without a sense of exclusivity about who can achieve what.

Third, we can ensure our 'all' outcome is challenging in itself, with the 'most' and 'some' outcomes then being even more challenging. This is a way to get round the idea the outcomes are differentiated in accordance with expectations regarding inherent ability. Instead, they are differentiated according to relative degrees of challenge – from challenging to very challenging.

My personal preference is for a combination of the first and third options. This sees us twice reinforcing high expectations to students. First through the outcomes we set, then by communicating that these are potentially accessible to everybody in the class.

When constructing your outcomes, begin with your objective. Work back from here and ask yourself what students will need to be able do to successfully meet the objective.

This illustrates why challenging objectives are so important. If they are too easy, the outcomes to which they give rise are not sufficiently challenging either.

It is possible to construct outcomes which reflect the taxonomy. For example, we might attach the level of analysis to our 'all' outcome, synthesis to our 'most' outcome and evaluation to our 'some' outcome. For example:

LO: To assess the arguments for and against the use of proportional representation

All will be able to apply arguments for and against in a piece of individual writing about proportional representation.

Most will be able to create a piece of writing which is balanced, taking into account both points of view.

Some will be able to rank the arguments on both sides as part of their writing, so as to come to a critical conclusion

This example has its merits. However, a clear limitation is that it suggests only those who reach the third outcome will be able to fully achieve the objective. This is a little problematic as it relies on us communicating to students that, although the outcomes are in the form All/Most/Some, the latter are still achievable by everybody in the class.

An alternative approach is to take the objective as the starting point, including the level of the taxonomy to which it refers, and to break this down into three levels of increasing complexity, each one tied to the level mentioned. Here is an example:

LO: To assess the arguments for and against the use of proportional representation

All will be able to assess the arguments for and against the use of proportional representation, explaining which side they think is more persuasive and why.

Most will be able to critically assess the arguments, suggesting why a range of opinions exist on the matter before giving their own perspective and supporting this with reasons, evidence and examples.

Some will be able to draw out the key concepts underpinning the arguments on each side and use these as the basis of a critical assessment of why different positions exist and whether or not these can be effectively reconciled.

The advantage of this approach is that each outcome sees the learning objective being met. The level at which it is met increases on each occasion. Those students who hit the third objective will be working at a very high level indeed.

The disadvantage is that the outcomes have become slightly more cumbersome and, as a result, a little harder to communicate to students.

I don't think there is a perfect solution to the problem. Both approaches to constructing outcomes have their benefits, but neither is perfect. The important thing to remember is that, whichever approach you choose, the outcomes should move up the taxonomy so as to ensure the pursuit of mastery remains integral to the lesson. In addition, having made yourself aware of the potential drawbacks of your chosen approach, you can then look to mitigate these either by, in the first case, helping students to see all the outcomes as accessible or, in the second case, carefully modelling and explaining the outcomes to aid student understanding.

Defining an Objective and Planning Backwards

In the previous sections we implied the benefits of defining an objective and planning backwards from there. Let us think about this in a bit more depth.

If we know the goal towards which our lesson is aiming, we are in a position to marshal our efforts squarely in pursuit of that goal. Given as how we are concerned with the application of Bloom's Taxonomy to lesson planning, that goal is likely to concern the development of mastery, or at least partial mastery, over the lesson content.

Having the objective defined means we can create a lesson more closely tied to helping students develop mastery than might otherwise be the case. This is because we can work back from the objective, including within the lesson all the steps necessary to ensure students are in a position to achieve it.

If we don't have an objective, or if our objective is ill-defined, it follows that the lesson elements we plan are less likely to achieve what we want them to achieve. They may do, or they may not; the chance of success is lowered by the lack of a clear goal towards which we can direct our efforts.

For example, if we define our learning objective as:

LO: To create an alternative ending to the story of Little Red Riding Hood

We can easily work back from here, identifying the various things students need to be able to do, know and understand in order to fulfil the objective. That these will mirror the levels of the taxonomy is inevitable, given what we have already said about the development of thinking and the use of the word 'create' in the objective.

First, students will need to know the story of Little Red Riding Hood, then they will need to understand how the plot works, be able to apply this understanding to different aspects of the story, and be able to compare the structure of the story to other stories with which they are familiar. When they have reached this point, they will be well placed to achieve the objective by creating an alternative ending of their own.

This example illustrates how a challenging objective based on one of the highest levels of the taxonomy can act as the peak of a pyramid, beneath which lies the foundations of learning which are layered up during the course of a lesson.

This again demonstrates why challenging objectives are so important. If we start with a simple, relatively easily to achieve objective, then we are going to be planning backwards from a fairly low end point, leading to less learning, smaller foundations and diminished progress.

It is worth noting that defining an objective from which to work backwards does not have to involve stating that objective in its final form. Some teachers find that codifying the objective at the start of the planning process can inhibit creative thinking. This is because the parameters of what is possible have been too closely defined (in their eyes) to allow exploration and development of different ideas.

However, teachers who choose not to fully state the objective at the beginning of the planning process are still likely to have a good idea in their minds of what the objective is – where they want students to be at the end of the lesson and how this relates to the taxonomy. That this is not fixed in a sentence or question does not mean that it doesn't exist. Rather, the teacher is choosing to allow themselves an element of leeway while they plan, which they feel wouldn't be available if the objective was fixed at the start.

This is a perfectly acceptable planning approach. The only risk is that, if you do not spend some time thinking through the general nature of your objective before you begin, then you may end up with a lesson which is somewhat uneven in its pursuit of mastery. This is because you will not have done enough analysis at the start to ensure you have a sufficiently clear idea of where you want the learning to go (even if this idea is not set in stone through the fixing of the objective in writing).

In summary, defining a challenging objective based on one of the top levels of the taxonomy is an excellent starting point for lesson planning. The definition can be full and fixed or partial and flexible. In the latter case, sufficient analytical thought should be done to ensure it retains its usefulness in directing and underpinning the lesson elements.

Tying Outcomes to Activities

Returning to outcomes, one of the ways in which these can be successfully achieved is by tying them to individual activities. Two possibilities are available for use.

The first sees us using separate activities for separate outcomes. So, for example, we might begin the lesson with an activity which focuses on our 'all' outcome, then move onto one which deals with our 'most' outcomes and then, finally, one which is concerned with our 'some' outcome.

The problem with this is that we risk seeing overall progress slow with each activity as groups of students drop away. This is because we have defined the outcomes as being accessible to all, most and some, not to everybody. Therefore, by the final activity we have a lesson which is focussed on the progress of the few rather than the many. Even if we stress that all outcomes are potentially achievable by all students, there is a likelihood that not all students will be able to engage successfully with the final activity.

A simple solution to this is as follows.

For each successive activity, *add an element* which deals exclusively with the next outcome, instead of planning an activity which *only* deals with the next outcome. This leads to a situation such as this:

Activity One – 'All' outcome

Activity Two – 'All' and 'Most' outcomes

Activity Three – 'All,' 'Most' and 'Some' outcomes

While this is a touch more challenging from the planning perspective, it is highly effective in maintaining good progress across the board in each lesson segment. The structure which results is inherently progressive (as each activity gets more challenging) while also allowing all students to access the learning at every stage (as each activity begins from the 'All' outcome).

One way to achieve this is by joining together subtasks based on different levels of the taxonomy, something we looked at earlier. Thus, Activity Two above would actually consist of two subtasks tied together, one aimed at the 'All' outcome and one aimed at the 'Most' outcome, both based on successive levels of the taxonomy. Activity Three would follow the same approach, except with three subtasks.

The second approach we might choose to follow involves planning a series of activities, each of which goes some way to meeting all three of the outcomes you have defined. This leads to a lesson in which students are able to work at different speeds throughout.

Three simple techniques to achieve such an end are as follows:

- Use the subtask approach but ensure that each activity you plan has three parts to it, each of which is tied to a different outcome and each of which is, as a result, more challenging than the previous part.

- Use extension tasks and questions as supplements to each activity you plan, with these giving access to the third and most challenging outcome ('Some...'). Here we are providing more-able students with work that pushes their thinking and helps them to achieve the most difficult outcome. However, we are also making the work available to all students (by, for example, displaying it on the board or on a resource), reinforcing the idea that targeted effort can help everybody to maximise their own progress.

- Give carefully delineated success criteria for each activity, with these criteria relating to your outcomes. So, for example, your first activity might come with five success criteria, the first two of which relate to the first outcome (all), the second two of which relate to the second (most) and the last of which relates to the third (some). In each activity, all students will have access to the various success criteria, but they won't necessarily achieve all of them. Instead, it is likely that students will reach the level of challenge which suits their current position. For example, one student might complete the first two success criteria but find the third a particular challenge, while another student might spend the majority of the activity trying to achieve the firth criterion.

Planning a Series of Objectives

When it comes to medium-term planning, that is, planning a unit, scheme of work or across the course of a term, it can be particularly helpful to begin by planning a series of objectives which together connect to the wider aims you have for students' learning.

Here is an example to illustrate the point:

I am sitting down to plan a unit of work looking at the Sociology of the Mass Media with my Year 11 GCSE class. My aims are threefold. First, I want to get them to a position where they are well-prepared to answer exam questions on the topic. Second, I want them to be able to connect their knowledge and understanding of the mass media to their wider sociological expertise. Third, I want to help them to critically analyse their own experiences of the mass media, including how it influences their identity.

You will note that these aims cover the instrumental aspects of teaching as well as the less prosaic ends.

Having defined my aims I now look at the time I have available. Let us imagine I have twelve lessons in which to cover the content set out in the exam board's specification. I divide it up accordingly, perhaps roughly at this point, and sit down to plan my twelve learning objectives.

This is where we hit upon another great advantage of using Bloom's Taxonomy to help us plan our lessons.

I have two routes to mastery which I want to pursue with my students. The first is a series of individual routes. That is, the lessons themselves. In each one I want students to make progress so they come to master the content about which we are learning. The second is the general route. That is, mastery in relation to those three aims I set out above. In this case, my intention is to construct a sequence of lessons which allow my students to achieve the overarching aims.

Using the taxonomy to plan a series of objectives in advance makes this relatively simple. First, I can go through my twelve lessons and, for each one, either specify a definite objective in the form of a statement or question, or do the analytical work necessary to gain a general idea of where I want to take students while still leaving myself the flexibility I might feel I need to be creative.

Next, I can review the objectives as a whole to see whether they also allow students to achieve the wider aims. If each one is sufficiently challenging and if I have made use of a range of keywords from the top levels of the taxonomy, it is likely this will be the case. If it isn't, however, I can go back and tinker with my objectives until I have them as I want.

For example, I might feel that I have fallen short in my desire to help students critically analyse their own experiences of mass media. Looking at my objectives I notice that I have prioritised the evaluation of sociological arguments concerning areas such as censorship, bias and the relationship between the media and the audience. I don't want to jettison any of this as it will help students gain mastery over these areas for use in the exam. However, I note that what I can do is broaden these objectives to encompass critical evaluation of the arguments as well as how these relate to people's experiences of the media, thus satisfying all three of the wider aims I outlined.

Approaching medium-term planning in this way helps sustain a level of challenge across a series of lessons while allowing you to achieve both your narrow, lesson-specific aims and your overarching ones. It also makes the subsequent planning of individual lessons simpler. This is for the reasons stated above regarding working backwards from objectives, but also because you can do you work safe in the knowledge that the bigger picture has been taken care of.

Using Outcomes to Promote Mastery

We will draw this chapter to a close by thinking further about how outcomes can be used to promote mastery in the medium-term.

Having followed the advice above and defined a set of challenging objectives across a series of lessons, with these carefully designed to meet our various aims, we are now in a position to think about our learning outcomes in the medium-term.

The process here is similar to that concerning objectives. By defining, loosely or specifically, the outcomes we want students to achieve during each lesson, we give ourselves a clear overview of how we intend to take them along the path to mastery.

We can review the map this creates, examining it to identify:

- Any gaps

- Any repetitions

- Any areas where challenge is not as great as we would like

- Whether or not the outcomes meet our lesson aims as well as our wider aims

- The extent to which we feel the outcomes will lead to excellent progress for all students

During this process, we critically assess the quality of the outcomes we settled on – or started to settle on if we are leaving them loosely defined until later in the course of our planning. This gives us the chance to sieve our ideas, refining them and intensifying their impact. Ultimately, this leads to lessons which are individually more effective and which, when brought together as a unit or scheme of work, help students to make more progress than would otherwise be the case.

It goes without saying that Bloom's Taxonomy is a major part of this process – as it is the taxonomy which has informed the creation of our outcomes, just as it has informed the creation of our objectives.

In conclusion, we can say the taxonomy is an essential tool on which we must call if we want to plan challenging objectives and outcomes. It provides a framework of mastery we can use to ensure this stage of our planning is effective and that it makes a suitable contribution towards our wider aim of maximising progress.

In the next chapter we will examine how using the taxonomy plays out when it comes to constructing activities, and how this can help us create lessons in which students meet or surpass the objectives and outcomes we plan.

Chapter Seven – Activities and Products

Bloom's Taxonomy is an excellent basis for activities, allowing you to construct tasks for your students which closely match their current level of mastery as well as helping them to progress to a higher level in relation to whatever content you are teaching. We have addressed this point already, thus our focus here will be on examples of specific activities you can use with your students.

At the end of the chapter we will also think about how we can use products as the basis of our lesson planning. This involves identifying the products we want students to produce (calling on the taxonomy to do this) before building our lessons around these.

Activities Overview

Activities are the building blocks of lessons. Along with the content we want students to learn about, they are the key element on which our teaching rests. Thought of in this way, we find ourselves with vessels (activities) into which relevant content is placed.

Many excellent activities exist. Some are subject-specific, others suitable for use across the curriculum. All remain similar in the sense that they ask students to do certain things with the lesson content. For our purposes, this doing is cognitive in basis.

Put another way, activities ask students to use different cognitive processes to interact with lesson content. As such, they are closely connected to the taxonomy.

A teacher may be aware of this or they may not. In the former case, we can imagine them planning a series of activities and recognising that these ask students to think in different ways, but not necessarily being familiar with the structure of complexity defined by the taxonomy.

This point intimates that having a good working knowledge of the taxonomy is beneficial when it comes to developing, applying and sequencing activities. If we know how the taxonomy works and appreciate the varying cognitive demands made by the different levels, then we are better placed to bend activities to our will; as opposed to using them without quite such a clear sense of purpose.

For example, it might be that one teacher plans a series of activities which they can see through their own analysis causes students to think increasingly critically about the topic of recycling. A second teacher, with a sound understanding of the taxonomy, is in a position to match this but to do so more quickly and with a greater sense of certainty, given their knowledge of how and why to apply the taxonomy for this particular purpose.

You don't have to understand the taxonomy to plan successful activities, but it helps.

Taking this point about speed, we can note two specific ways in which familiarity allows us to plan quickly and effectively. First, we do not need to spend a great deal of time trying to work out a series of activities which are progressively more challenging. We can simply turn to the taxonomy for our framework. Second, if we devise an activity and are uncertain as to the relative level of challenge it promotes, we need not agonise. Instead, we can compare it to the taxonomy, make a judgement and then, if necessary, alter it.

Leading on from the previous chapter, here is an example of how we might plan quickly and effectively.

Having settled on a learning objective and a series of learning outcomes, we continue our planning by writing down a formulation such as the following:

Starter: Knowledge

First Activity: Comprehension

Second Activity: Application

Third Activity: Analysis/Evaluation

Plenary: Reflection

In but a moment we have a progressive, challenging framework for our lesson which allows us to push student learning across the board. Another option we might choose to use is:

Starter: Knowledge/Comprehension

First Activity: Knowledge/Comprehension/Application

Second Activity: Comprehension/Application/Analysis

Third Activity: Application/Analysis/Synthesis

Plenary: Reflection

This reflects that different formulation we outlined in the previous chapter, where we seek to give opportunities to work towards all outcomes in all sections of the lesson.

Either of these approaches gives us a skeleton for our lessons, one we can use as the basis for students learning about and interacting with the relevant content, with this happening through the activities we choose at each stage.

A final point to note in this overview is that there may be occasions, particularly when first introducing a topic, where we need to spend longer on the lower levels of the taxonomy. In Science, for example, it may be necessary that students know and comprehend a large amount of content before they are in a position to apply it. In such situations, we can still call on a swiftly expressed Bloom's-based framework. The only difference will be that we do not seek to scale multiple levels in a single lesson, instead choosing to do this over the course of a few lessons, due to the nature of the content.

I mention this here because it is a situation with which many of us will be familiar, and because it presents a corrective to the view, which might have been implied, that the two outlines I suggest above are suitable for all lessons. Certainly, they are suitable for many, but this does not mean they are suitable for all.

Nonetheless, the point remains that thinking about lesson structure from the perspective of the taxonomy allows for quick sketching of the outline of a lesson, as well as increased certainty about the progressive nature of that sketch, and a sense of confidence about the direction in which each activity ought to take the learning.

Knowledge and Comprehension Activities

In this section and the next two, I will outline a range of exemplar activities suitable for use in a range of contexts.

We begin with **knowledge**:

1. Ask students to create a list of things connected to the topic. This could be recalled information or it could be new information you want students to learn. In the latter case, you should provide the resources such as textbooks or handouts from which students can extract the information.

To help students separate out pieces of information you might provide a series of headings under which lists can be made. Alternatively, you might divide the class into groups, give each group a different area about which to make their lists and then bring everyone back together to share their findings.

2. Ask students to create mind-maps showing what they already know about a topic. Mind-maps are useful because they allow students to recall and visualise connections as well as single pieces of information. They can also be referred to during the course of a lesson. For example, students might make a Macbeth mind-map and use this as a thinking aid during a series of more challenging activities. Spider diagrams, brainstorms and concept maps all represent variations on this theme.

3. Ask students to create a chart showing what they know about the topic of study. The design of the chart can be left to students or you can provide a pro-forma for them to use. In the latter case, you can create something which helps students collate information in a way you think most useful.

A nice benefit of information charts is that students can return to them over a series of lessons, adding new information on each occasion. This helps them to see how their knowledge is developing, acts as a memory aid, and also affords students the chance to make links and connections.

4. Ask students to make a timeline, glossary, storyboard or other such summary of relevant information. Timelines, glossaries and storyboards are examples of specific ordering devices through which we can sequence and record information with which we are familiar. Different devices have different uses.

A time line, for example, has greater relevance in History than in Art, just as a glossary will probably be more use in Psychology than in Music (though it depends a little on the level at which the subject is being studied). The point is that different ordering devices are more or less relevant for different subjects and areas of study.

Now for some **comprehension** activities:

1. Set students a series of questions about the knowledge they have developed. These questions should focus on student understanding, asking them to explain, demonstrate and illustrate that which they have come to know. The aim is to give students a chance to convey their understanding. As they think about what they know, how they know it and what it means to communicate this clearly, so they refine their understanding.

2. Ask students to communicate their knowledge through a different medium or form. For example, if students have made a list of all the key facts about volcanoes, you might then ask them to explain how volcanoes work through a diagram or through a voiceover script for a television documentary.

The process of translating information from one form to another will help students to develop their understanding; it will also challenge them to take the various pieces of information they know and put them together into some sort of a whole, with this whole (the diagram or script, for example) being the vehicle they use to communicate their understanding.

3. Ask students to put the information about which they have learned into their own words. This means students have to go beyond the simple recall involved in copying out or writing down verbatim what has been remembered. Instead, the pieces of information have to be brought together into an explanation which is the student's own; which shows their understanding.

Some students struggle with this. To help them, you might provide guidance by specifying the various topics successive sentences or paragraphs should cover. This divides up the cognitive load, providing students with a structure and allowing them to focus all their efforts on getting the content right.

4. If students have been learning about a process or a series of events, ask them to produce a flowchart demonstrating the nature of this. Here, students have to separate out and order the different pieces of information they have learned. Doing this helps them to better understand the process or sequence. They will then be able to communicate this understanding through their flowchart.

You can press for further comprehension by asking students to annotate their flowcharts with explanations of specific points as well as of the relationships between things (such as how one causes another).

Application and Analysis Activities

Now we move up the taxonomy, turning our attention to **application**:

1. Set students the task of solving problems with which they are not familiar but which connect to the topic they are studying. The lack of familiarity is key as it is this which causes students to apply the knowledge and understanding they have gained. If problems are familiar then students may simply recall solutions, which does not help develop their understanding.

A good approach is to present a series of progressively more complex or esoteric problems. This creates an enhanced sense of progression, with students having to work harder to effectively apply what they know and understand to each subsequent problem.

2. A variation on the theme of problem-solving is that of scenarios. These are a specific type of problem, usually connected to the real-world (albeit, they might be imagined), in which students have to use their knowledge and understanding to work out the best way forward. A simple example is that of: What would you do in this situation and why?

A more challenging example involves us setting students an unfamiliar scenario containing a range of variables and asking them to apply their knowledge to this. For example, we might be teaching about climate change and present students with a case study looking at a developing country's industrial policy before asking them to apply their knowledge of developing countries and of renewable energy to the problem of lowering the country's emissions while maintaining economic growth.

3. Ask students to explain why certain things are the case. These things should be connected to the lesson topic but should not be familiar to students. The aim is to create a situation in which students are applying their knowledge and understanding to explain or demonstrate something unfamiliar.

For example, we might teach students about the meaning of forgiveness in Christian theology before presenting them with a range of examples of Christian figures who chose to forgive or not to forgive. We would then ask them to explain why each one of the figures made their choice and whether it fits with the theology. This sees students applying their understanding in search of an answer.

4. As a final example, we might set up 'live' situations in which students need to apply their understanding in order to proceed. For example, in a PE lesson we might teach a skill and then move students into a series of small-scale games in which they have to try to apply that skill. Or, we might demonstrate a mathematical procedure before giving students a selection of equations they must aim to solve by applying the procedure.

These are both examples of active practice, where students gain a basic knowledge and understanding of something – in these cases a skill and a procedure – which they then develop by applying it again and again in a short space of time.

Next, our focus moves to **analysis**:

1. Present students with something they must investigate or test. This could be a hypothesis, a statement or a question. If the latter, it should be sufficiently open to warrant sustained analysis. Questions of this type are enquiry questions – in as much as they provoke the respondent into a period of enquiry.

You can structure the process of analysis encouraged by such an activity in a number of ways. First, you can give students a series of sub-questions which they must answer as part of their work. Second, you can divide the task into separate subtasks and indicate that by completing each one in turn the desired results will arrive. Third, by giving success criteria which illustrate the manner in which the analysis ought to take place. This is particularly relevant if the investigation needs to mirror a certain method – such as is seen in the sciences.

2. Ask students to examine a particular thing and to produce a report detailing their findings. There is a closeness between examination and investigation. The former, however, is less directed than the latter and can be used in a wider variety of situations. Consider how a doctor might examine a patient to see their present condition whereas they would be likely to investigate a specific complaint.

An example of examination is in English Literature, where we might provide students with a poem and ask them to examine its structure, the author's use of imagery and the effect it has upon the reader. Here we are giving a structure to the examination by specifying the areas we believe to be of greatest importance. We can increase the level of challenge by asking students to first decide what they think the examination should focus on and to then justify this decision.

3. Ask students to work in pairs and provide them with material which is relevant to the topic – for example a selection of sources in History, some test results in Chemistry or a collection of product designs in DT. Explain they need to look at the range of things they have been given and, in so doing, identify any patterns, trends, similarities or differences.

This is a developed version of compare and contrast, with students challenged through the provision of multiple items and multiple areas to look at. The aim is to encourage the development of a nuanced understanding of the variations which might be present in a given topic. This helps increase the depth and complexity of students' understanding.

4. Provide students with a topic and ask them to work individually or in groups to research this. You might want to use a research question instead of a general topic, or you might leave it up to your students to create a question based on the topic you set.

One of the risks of setting a research task is that students get bogged down trying to wade through an excess of information. You can help them avoid this by modelling at the start of the task how to narrow down your focus so as to effectively discriminate between what is useful and what is not during the course of the task. This involves showing students how to identify and then apply criteria connected to the research topic/question. For example, whether or not a piece of information is directly or tangentially connected to the area of interest. It is an example of you modelling thinking for your students.

Synthesis and Evaluation Activities

Finally, we reach the top of the taxonomy. First up is **synthesis**:

1. Ask students to create something which allows them to call on a wide range of previously developed knowledge and understanding. For example, you might ask them to create a guide, leaflet or presentation, an essay, poster, sequence of lessons, report or piece of individual writing. Essentially, any reasonably large product is appropriate as long as it involves the manipulation and bringing together of disparate pieces of information and rests on the understanding students have developed.

Our aim is to give students an opportunity to use what they know and understand to create something new. This will tie closely to the lesson topic. The scope of what a Physics lesson might lead a student to create is different from that of an Art lesson. To this end, while certain products can be the basis of a creation task in a range of subjects, other products will only be suitable for certain subjects.

2. Challenge students to develop a design which takes their existing knowledge and understanding as a starting point but then moves off from this to suggest something new. Examples of design tasks include designing an alternative, designing a solution, designing a different version, designing a prototype, designing an experiment, designing a test, designing an interpretation and designing an advertising campaign.

In each case, students need to draw together the separate elements of what they know and use these as the basis for the new construction. This is challenging but also tends to be highly stimulating and motivational. For students who might struggle with synthesis in general, exemplar work is particularly useful here. Such models provide a great starting point for these students, scaffolding the act of designing (or creating), and increasing the likelihood they will be able to engage with task at length.

3. Ask students to merge together different ideas or pieces of information to create a complete whole. For example, we might ask students to develop a series of arguments connected to a relevant statement (analysis) and to then bring these together to form an essay. Or, we might ask students to take something which exists (such as a model of the water cycle) and to merge this with another idea or piece of information (such as a model of how industrial pollution contaminates sources of freshwater) to create a whole which is greater than the sum of its parts.

As you will note, I have returned here to using the word 'create.' Despite this, activities based on the idea of merging are qualitatively different from those based just on creation (see above). This is because merging tends to refer to the coming together of two or more different elements to form a new whole. Create, on the other hand, retains a broader meaning and does not presuppose the maintenance of elements in the way that merge implies.

4. Ask students to plan a response to a question or challenge. Depending on what this is, there may also be the opportunity for students to implement their plan. However, it is the development of the plan which is itself the act of synthesis and, as a result, doing this even without having the opportunity for implementation will be beneficial for their progress.

For example, in a Religious Studies lesson looking at Buddhism we might ask students to plan a school event introducing parents to the key teachings of the Buddha. We could caveat this with a challenge by asking students to think about how they could make the event interactive and how they could ensure parents don't develop any misconceptions as they take part. This illustrates how planning tasks can be made more or less difficult through the use of additional demands.

We now come to our last port of call, **evaluation**:

1. Challenging students to assess something means asking them to look at it in the light of their knowledge and understanding and to make a judgement. For assess-based tasks to be effective, that which is being assessed needs to be clear and, ideally, to have a sufficient degree of depth for a detailed decision to be arrived at.

For example, in a PE theory lesson we might ask students to assess the quality of a proposed exercise programme designed to promote muscle gain. Here, students would have a number of elements to consider when making their assessment, including the elements of which the programme is constituted and the extent to which these together will lead to muscle gain.

Self- and peer-assessment are also relevant to this point. In both cases, students are being asked to use their knowledge and understanding of the topic, as well as what good work looks like, to come to some sort of judgement. Both these activities are most effective if the teacher takes time to train students in what to look for concerning the latter, in how to successfully use mark-schemes or success criteria to pass judgements, and how to go from this to providing feedback.

2. Ask students to critique an idea, interpretation, experiment, design, piece of writing or something else. Critique differs from assess in that the emphasis is more explicitly negative. While assessment tends to involve the weighing up of strengths and weaknesses, critiquing generally errs towards drawing out the various problems or limitations inherent within something.

For example, having spent a lesson looking at how to develop a healthy, balanced food menu, we might then present students with a selection of possible menus which it is their job to critique in the light of what they have learned. This critique will focus on identifying the problems in each menu, with any points raised having to be justified with reference to the knowledge and understanding developed during the course of the lesson.

3. The reverse of critique is defend. When we ask students to defend something we ask them to pull out all the strengths connected to the thing in question, as well as the benefits and the points of interest which set it apart from similar thinks of its ilk. The process of defending a proposition, argument, idea, design approach or method involves students building a case for the item in question. In so doing they need to invoke all they have learned and understood. This gives them the framework through which they can make their positive judgements and, crucially, attempt to persuade others of their worthiness.

For example, we might ask a group of Psychology students to defend the psychodynamic explanation of aggression. In doing this, they are compelled to build up a picture of the relative strengths of this explanation, even if they do not agree with it.

A nice use of defence-style tasks is to divide the class into teams and give each team a different, competing thing to defend. This adds a sense of competition and fun, with students working against each other to persuade the teacher (or the class as a whole) that whatever they have been asked to defend is, indeed, the best of the lot.

Extending the example above, we might divide the class into three and ask one team to defend the psychodynamic explanation of aggression, another team to defend the biological explanation and a third to defend the explanation provided by social learning theory.

Two final points to note. First, this same development (competing teams) can be used as part of a critique-based activity. Second, critique and defend can be combined, with teams asked to defend whatever they have been given and, in the process, critique the positions of their opponents. This is more challenging as it requires students to attend to both sides of evaluation at once. It can also lead to some impassioned debates!

4. We finish this section by looking at ranking activities. You can call on these at various points of the lesson but they will tend to produce better results if used nearer the end. This is because students will have had sufficient time in which to develop their knowledge and understanding of the topic, leading them to make more detailed, thoughtful judgements regarding the ranking of different items.

Two things need to be considered in any ranking activity: what is being ranked and how it is being ranked. For the former, almost anything is possible – arguments, ideas, approaches, factors, possible solutions, plans, theories and so on. For the latter, a smaller range of possibilities tend to present themselves. For example: from most to least useful, from most to least likely, from most to least relevant, from strongest to weakest, and so on.

When students engage in ranking activities, they may be tempted to rank the items in question and then leave it at that. But this is only half the job! To get the most out of the activity in cognitive terms, we must encourage students to provide a clear rationale for the decision they have come to regards the ranking. They must justify their choices, calling on their knowledge and understanding of the content to do so.

A few variations on straightforward ranking are worth noting. First, is the use of a 'diamond 9' approach. This is where we ask students to rank nine items in levels of 1, 2, 3, 2, and 1. This presents a different proposition as students have to decide which items they view as equal and what it takes for an item to be ranked on a level above or beneath another.

Second, is the repeated use of a ranking activity during a lesson or over a course of lessons. Here we take students back to their original rankings on a series of occasions to see whether further learning has caused them to change their minds or not. Of course, whether it has or hasn't, they must still justify their position.

Third, is the double-rank approach. Here, we first ask students to rank a selection of items in accordance with one set of criteria, before introducing a second set and asking students to assess whether their rankings change as a result. This can be particularly useful in helping students to see familiar material in a different light.

Products

We finish our section on activities by turning matters around and thinking about products – the things activities ask students to create.

In all the examples above, different products result from what we ask students to do. By turning this on its head we move from first defining our objectives and outcomes to asking the question: What do we want students to be able to produce, either at the end of the lesson or at the end of each activity, to demonstrate they have made the best progress possible?

Thinking in this way means subjugating the process of lesson planning to the end products, rather than to the activities or the content. This approach it is not for everybody. However, it does have certain benefits.

Thinking about products means identifying what success will look like in highly tangible terms in any given activity or lesson. For example, we might have a lesson objective as follows:

LO: To investigate the most effective way to limit coastal erosion

We might decide that, come the end of our lesson, we want students to be able to stand up in front of the class and deliver a two-minute speech outlining the different ways coastal erosion can be limited before indicating which method they favour and why.

Or, we might decide students should be able to produce a reasonably detailed decision tree they can use to work out the best method of limiting coastal erosion in the most common situations.

Here we can see that the product we define as the endpoint will be based on the higher levels of the taxonomy, given as how these processes give rise to products of the greatest cognitive depth. In addition, it is notable that having so defined a worthwhile, in-depth product, we then find our decision-making cast beneath the light of this. Taking the two examples above, it is plain that whichever we settle on, subtly different – perhaps widely different – lessons will come about as a result.

Another advantage of beginning with products is that we immediately have a lens through which to view the different activities we intend to plan. If I want students to be able to produce a detailed coastal erosion decision tree by the end of the lesson then I will need to plan a starter activity and one or two follow-up activities which give them the requisite knowledge and understanding to do this.

The same point could be made about learning objectives in general – that they are a lens through which to make decisions. The difference with products is that the lens is sharpened because a highly specific end has been decided upon. Some teachers like to work in this way, while others feel it limits their ability to be creative.

A final benefit of beginning with the end product is that you can opt for product types which you think will particularly suit your students, or which will fit well with the topic you are teaching. Of course, such a benefit is not limited to this approach – similar decisions can be made in other circumstances – but if the product is the first port of call, thinking in this way is a little easier than if you have already planned your activities and then find yourself needing to make adaptations to ensure you get the end product you really want.

To conclude this brief foray into products and the taxonomy, here is list of products to which your lessons can give rise:

Advertisement
Annotated bibliography
Art gallery
Biography
Blueprint
Board game
Book Cover
Brochure
Bulletin board
Card or board game

Chart
Collage
Collection with illustration
Collection with narrative
Comic Strip
Computer program
Crossword puzzle
Debate
Detailed illustration
Diary
Diorama
Display
Drama
Dramatic monologue
Editorial
Essay
Experiment
Experiment Log
Fable
Fact file
Fairy tale
Family tree
Glossary
Graph
Graphic design
Greeting card
Illustrated story
Journal
Labeled diagram
Large scale drawing
Lecture
Letter
Letter to the editor
Lesson
Line drawing
Magazine article
Map

Map with legend
Mobile sculpture
Museum exhibit
Musical composition
News report
Pamphlet
Pattern with instructions
Photo essay
Picture dictionary
Podcast
Poem
Poster
Reference file
PowerPoint Presentation
Survey
Video
Vocabulary List
Written report

This non-exhaustive list was taken from
http://cs1.mcm.edu/~awyatt/csc3315/bloom.htm some years ago,
however the webpage is no longer accessible.

Chapter Eight – Questioning

Questioning is one of the most important tools at the teacher's disposal. We ask hundreds of questions every day – it is perhaps the primary way that we communicate with students. The quality of the questions we ask has a direct impact on the progress students make. By asking better questions we can stimulate better progress. In this chapter we will look at the role Bloom's Taxonomy can play in helping you to ask great questions.

Questioning Overview

Questions make demands of the people to whom they are posed. In our case, they make demands of students. These demands are generally cognitive – we ask students to think in certain ways, to engage in certain mental operations – and, as such, closely tied to learning.

If we only ask questions which demand simple cognitive processes, or ask students to guess rather than to think, then we are failing to maximise the amount of learning which goes on in our classrooms. It is for this reason that we should pay attention to the questions we ask, rather than relying on thinking up good questions on the spot or hoping those we ask are just good enough.

The taxonomy, with its clear delineation of cognitive processes and its framework for mastery learning, is a useful tool we can use to structure our questions. No matter what prior learning a student possesses, or what level they find themselves at relative to the curriculum or to their peers, we can use the taxonomy to support them through our questioning, to challenge them and to help them to make rapid progress.

An easy way in which you can start using the taxonomy to inform your questioning is to print off a list of the keywords connected to each level (see Chapter Two) and stick this to your desk or to your classroom wall. Straightaway you will have an aide memoire to which you can refer when asking questions.

So, for example, if you do not have sufficient time to plan your questions prior to a lesson, you can instead look to your list of keywords while you are teaching and use these as the basis of the questions you ask. Doing this makes it easier for you to pose challenging questions. It also makes it easier to pose questions connected to your students' current knowledge and understanding.

Another helpful approach is to sit down and develop a suite of staple questions, connected to the subject or age-group you teach, based on the different levels of the taxonomy (or, you might prefer to focus on the top three or four levels). You can print these questions out, laminate the list and keep it to hand as a scaffold for yourself. Over time, as you have the opportunity to practice asking these questions, you will come to internalise them. Eventually, the scaffold will become superfluous and you will be able to rely on your memory.

These strategies represent our first forays into how to use the taxonomy to ensure great questioning. In the rest of the chapter we will look at a range of further techniques and strategies on which we can call.

Question Stems

Question stems are the beginning parts of questions. These are the command sections indicating what process we would like the respondent to engage in. They are accompanied by the subject part of the question, which indicates the content we would like the respondent to apply the process to. Question stems are generic and can be used in a range of situations. Subject sections are specific and vary depending on the topic of study.

Here are some examples to demonstrate:

What caused the Great Depression?

How would you characterise an oxbow lake?

To what extent do you agree that fairness is more important than justice?

The questions stems are:

What caused…

How would you characterise…

To what extent do you agree…

We could take these stems and use them in a wide range of contexts. This means that, if we develop a well-conceived set of question stems, using the taxonomy as our basis, we can use these to construct good questions in most settings.

Here are a selection of such stems for each level of the taxonomy:

Knowledge Question Stems

What happened after…?
How many…?
Who was it that…?
Can you name the…?
Describe what happened at…?
Who spoke to…?
Can you tell why…?
Find the meaning of…?
What is…?
Which is true or false…?

Comprehension Question Stems

Can you write in your own words...?
Can you write a brief outline...?
What do you think might have happened next...?
Who do you think...?
What was the main idea...?
Who was the key character...?
Can you distinguish between...?
What differences exist between...?
Can you provide an example of what you mean...?
Can you provide a definition for...?

Application Question Stems

Do you know another instance where...?
Could this have happened in...?
Can you group by characteristics such as...?
What factors would you change if...?
Can you apply the information to...?
What questions would you ask...?
From the information, can you develop a set of instructions about...?
Would this information be useful if you had...?

Analysis Question Stems

Which events could have happened...?
How was this similar to...?
What was the underlying theme of...?
Would it work if...?
Why did...changes occur?
Can you compare your...with that presented in...?
Can you explain what must have happened when...?
How is...similar to...?
What are some of the problems of...?
Can you distinguish between...?

What were some of the motives behind...?
What was the turning point in...?
What was the problem with...?

Synthesis Question Stems

Can you design...?
Can you see a possible solution to...?
If you had access to a complete set of resources, how would you deal with...?
Why don't you devise your own way to deal with...?
What would happen if...?
How many ways can you...?
Can you create new use for...?
What might an alternative...look like?
Can you propose how we would...?

Evaluation Question Stems

Is there a better solution to...?
Can you assess the value of...?
Can you defend your position about...?
Do you think...is a good or a bad thing? Why?
How would you have handled...?
What changes to...would you recommend?
Do you believe...?
How would you feel if...?
How effective are...?
What do you think about...?

These lists were taken from
http://www.teachers.ash.org.au/researchskills/Dalton.htm some years ago, though the site is not currently accessible; I have made some minor changes.

The lists as a whole provide a valuable starting point, though they are not exhaustive. You can use them to develop your own questions and your own question stems. Another great advantage of having a list of question stems is that you can share these with students. They can then use the stems to come up with their own questions, which they ask to you, to themselves or to each other.

A final point to note is that if you are teaching an exam class, it is likely the questions set by the exam board will be based on a limited range of question stems, with these linked to the levels of the taxonomy. To speed up the process of exam preparation, you can analyse past papers to identify the relevant question stems, before making a list of these and using them regularly during the course of your lessons. This familiarises students with the question types they are likely to meet, as well as the best ways in which to respond to these.

Tailored Questioning

Tailored questioning is where we adapt and modify our questions so they more closely meet the needs of the students to whom we are asking them. If we want to question effectively, we would unlikely consider it sensible to ask the same questions to all students at all times. Such an approach fails to take account of the differences in students' knowledge and understanding.

However, tailoring questions is not easy. First, we need a reasonably accurate idea of where students are at, then we need to understand where we want to take their learning before, finally, creating a question or series of questions which allow us to achieve this.

For the first part, understanding where students are at, we need to ask diagnostic questions. That is, questions which elicit the information necessary for us to appreciate what students know and what they don't know, what they can do and what they can't do, and what they understand as well as what they don't understand.

The taxonomy provides an excellent basis for this. We can pose questions based on the levels we think appropriate to the student in question. For example, we might start with a series of comprehension question before moving onto application and ascertaining that this is where the student in question is running into trouble.

Depending on the answers you elicit, you can move up the taxonomy more quickly or more slowly until you find the point of challenge for the student in question. Having found it, you can then pursue this, calling on question stems such as those listed above to help you form the questions which will push students' thinking, or help them to unlock ideas with which they are struggling.

In summary, the method works as follows:

- Remind yourself of the taxonomy

- Ask students questions which rise up the levels of the taxonomy

- Stop when you hit a level with which students have difficulty

- Pursue this by asking questions at or around this level which promote thinking and/or help to unlock understanding for students

Using the taxonomy in this way means we are consistently applying the idea of mastery learning and the delineation of cognitive processes to our questioning. In so doing, our questions become closely tied to the needs and understanding of the students we teach. This leads to better outcomes and faster progress across the board.

Framing Lessons and Activities

We mentioned in Chapter Six the benefits which come from framing learning objectives as questions. The technique encourages a sense of enquiry, provides a means to judge progress through the course of the lesson and engages students to seek answers to the questions we pose.

We can also use questions to frame the lesson as a whole and to underpin individual activities. For example, we might give our lesson a title in the form of a question and then present a learning objective such as: 'To produce a detailed, reasoned answer to the question by the end of the lesson.'

Here, we are communicating to students from the moment they enter the room that we are engaged in a shared endeavour and that the endeavour is concerned with the development of our understanding.

Another option is to have sub-questions as activity titles. This sees students working through a task to try to answer the question which has been set. Frequently, students find this motivational. The answering of the question becomes an end towards which the activity aims; achieving the goal is a mission students want to fulfil.

To develop challenging, engaging questions in both these cases we can turn to the taxonomy. Earlier, we looked at how we might break a lesson down into a series of separate activities with each activity being based on one or more levels of the taxonomy.

If we take this route, it is easy to use questions to frame activities. We simply take the activity we have planned, remind ourselves of the level(s) of the taxonomy to which it refers, and shape a question accordingly – perhaps using the question stems outlined above.

In terms of framing the lesson as a whole, we might first write a learning objective and set of outcomes based on the taxonomy (as explained previously) and then pare these down into a single question which, if answered effectively, will allow students to display the knowledge and understanding they have developed during the course of the lesson.

Finally, it is worth noting that the framing of lessons can be extended to the framing of an entire topic. Here, we set an overarching question concerned with the topic as a whole. To ensure a high level of challenge, this is based on one of the top levels of the taxonomy. Then, we plan a series of separate questions which, if answered, will allow us to answer the wider question. These separate questions form the basis of our individual lessons. For example:

Topic Question: To what extent is Marxism an outmoded and outdated theory of society?

Lesson One Question: What characterises Marxist explanations of society?

Lesson Two Question: How do Marxist explanations compare to other theories?

Lesson Three Question: Is it possible to modify Marxism to fit with the modern world?

Lesson Four Question: To what extent does Marxism overemphasise the role of class?

Lesson Five Question: Why do some sociologists still use Marxism as the basis of their work?

Lesson Six Question: How can we best assess the various critiques of Marxist thought?

By focussing on the higher levels of the taxonomy in the construction of the questions and by planning the lesson questions through the lens of the topic question, we have produced the outline of a challenging, enquiry-based unit of work. We can apply the approach to medium-term planning in any area of the curriculum or with any age-group.

Students Asking and Creating Questions

This is something we want. If it happens regularly then students are consistently thinking about the topic from critical, analytical and creative perspectives. This is because all three of these approaches are inherent in the development of questions.

We cannot ask a question without being at least partly analytical or creative. Students who are encouraged to ask and develop questions of their own are thus encouraged to exercise their faculties in pursuit of greater understanding and improved mastery.

One strategy we can employ is to share Bloom's-based question stems with our students, as noted above.

Another approach is to ask students to predict what questions they think they will be able to answer at the end of a lesson or unit of work and to then come back to these through the course of our teaching. On each occasion we can ask students to reflect on whether they stand by their original predictions in light of their subsequent learning or whether they would look to change these.

An unusual but effective technique is to plan a plenary activity in which the class is split in half, with one group charged with developing synthesis-based questions connected to the learning while the other group create evaluation-based ones. Pairs are then formed, consisting of one member from each group. Finally, students test each other's knowledge and understanding by taking it in turns to pose the questions they developed.

Another strategy works as follows. At the end of a unit of work, divide the class into an even number of teams. Display Bloom's Taxonomy on the board along with example question stems or explanations for each level. Explain that teams have fifteen minutes to produce a twelve question quiz they will use to test the knowledge and understanding of their peers. Indicate that quizzes should contain two questions connected to each of the six levels of the taxonomy. When the time is up, ask groups to pair up, swap quizzes and try to answer the questions posed by their peers. A variation involves the teacher selecting one team at random who then pose their questions to the class as a whole.

Our final technique is best used at the start of a unit of work. Provide students with a hand-out containing six boxes. Each box should have a different level of the taxonomy as a title. Give students some guidance, explanation or examples as to the meaning of the different levels. Next, introduce the topic of study and invite students to fill their sheets with questions they want to be able to answer by the time they complete the unit of work.

At the start of each lesson, ask students to retrieve their sheets, tick off any questions they can now answer and add in any new ones they have identified.

At the end of the unit, invite students to go through their sheets and check they can answer all their questions – they might also like to swap sheets with a partner to see if there are questions they have missed.

Extension Questions

We will look at stretch and challenge in detail in Chapter Ten. Here, we can think briefly about using the taxonomy to structure extension questions. These questions are supplements to the main work of the lesson. They are called extensions because they are intended to extend the thinking of those students who get onto them.

For this reason, the top three levels of the taxonomy are of most use whenever we plan such questions. These levels make the greatest cognitive demands on students; something we want to be doing if we are seeking to extend thinking.

Here are three approaches you can use to plan extension questions:

- Plan a set of extension questions based on evaluation and synthesis which are relevant to your subject and/or age-group and which can be called upon again and again in a range of different situations. Such questions might be generic in design, or they might be question stems into which you fit different subjects. Either way, the aim is to have a selection of questions on which you can call without the need for much additional planning, meaning you are always ready to challenge students' thinking.

- When students complete an activity, present them with a list of keywords (analysis, synthesis, evaluation or all three) alongside a couple of example questions. Challenge them to create and then answer their own extension question. As an alternative, if more than one student has completed the activity, you can ask students to create extension questions which they then pose to each other – this creates a nice sense of competition and also means the students in question have a subsequent opportunity to discuss their questions and answers with each other.

- Create a range of extension questions you can apply across the topics you teach. You can come up with these yourself or you can turn the exercise into an activity by inviting students to help you develop a wide range (scaffold by providing word lists relating to the top levels of the taxonomy). Write each question on a slip of paper. Fold these up and store them in a shoe box (or something similar). When students complete the main activity, ask them to choose an extension question from the shoe box. This creates a nice sense of theatre around the process, increasing motivation and engagement (you might also like to decorate the shoebox to further liven things up!).

Stepped Questioning

A useful activity you can develop based around the taxonomy is stepped questioning. This is where we present students with a series of questions which gradually move up the levels and, as a result, become increasingly challenging. Here is an example:

1. What can you remember about the video? **(Knowledge)**

2. How would you explain the plot of the film? **(Comprehension)**

3. How could you use the plot to explain real-life situations? **(Application)**

4. What motivated the main characters to behave as they did? **(Analysis)**

5. If you could rewrite the film, how would you make it different? **(Synthesis)**

6. Do you agree the film is overly sentimental? Why? **(Evaluation)**

Question one is the simplest, questions five and six the most challenging. The framework is clear: a set of questions, each a step up, in terms of the cognitive demands they make, from the previous one.

You can present a set of questions like this as a single activity, with students working individually or in pairs to answer them. Such an activity is differentiated because there is an expectation that some students will get further than others, depending on the prior knowledge and understanding with which they meet the questions.

Another option is to pose a series of questions like this verbally. This sees us working with individual students, pairs or small groups and asking them a series of stepped questions with the aim of developing knowledge and understanding. The discussions which ensue allow us to push student thinking. If we know the taxonomy off-by-heart, we can come up with a set of stepped questions off the cuff, tailoring these to the needs of the students with whom we are talking.

Circulating and Intervening

Highly effective activities afford us the opportunity to circulate through the class. While doing this we can elicit information about student learning – by observing, listening, reading work and through discussion.

One of the best ways to use this information is by posing questions which cause students to think differently about the lesson content, or which cause them to think in ways they might otherwise have ignored.

For example, we might observe a group of students labouring under a misconception as they attempt to complete a piece of group work. We would then intervene and pose a question which helps reveal why this is a misconception. This leads into a discussion in which we direct students' thinking towards a more accurate understanding of the information in question.

When circulating, Bloom's Taxonomy is a useful tool on which we can call. This is for three reasons.

First, when eliciting information about student learning, we can compare this to our knowledge of the taxonomy. Through doing this, we can quickly and easily ascertain what the information we have elicited means in the context of the student's mastery. For example, we might note that the discussion they are having with their peer is fairly analytical, allowing us to judge that their understanding is at a reasonably high level.

Second, when intervening in response to the information we have elicited, we can base this intervention on the taxonomy. So, to continue the example from above, we might pose a question to the students involved in this analytical discussion which challenges them to think more evaluatively about the lesson content. Here, we are basing our intervention on a comparison between the information we have elicited and our pre-existing knowledge of the taxonomy. This allows us to maximise the effectiveness of our intervention.

Third, we can make judgements about the class as a whole by circulating through the entire room and comparing what we find out to our knowledge of the taxonomy, as well as to the intentions we had when we used it to plan the lesson. We are interested in assessing the extent to which our teaching is achieving the kind of progress we want. If it is, we can feel happy our efforts have been effective. If it is not, we can review the information we have elicited in light of the taxonomy and make a judgement about how best to proceed. For example, we might decide the best option is to take the whole class back to an earlier question concerned with analysis, which we thought they had grasped, and to spend some more time examining this and thinking about what it means before trying to move on any further.

Concrete to Abstract Questioning

We are familiar with the way in which the taxonomy characterises the different cognitive processes as being steps on a path to mastery. Another way to think about it is as a continuum which, roughly, runs from more concrete to more abstract thought.

Knowledge and comprehension is concerned with the recall and explanation of facts – of information we have concerning the world. Application and analysis sees us using what we know. Here we are beginning to engage in more abstract cognition because we are starting from our understanding, rather than from the world itself. Finally, synthesis and evaluation ask us to manipulate our already reasonably abstract thoughts to a further degree, meaning that these two levels are like a second remove from the first phase of concrete recall and explanation.

This gives a different perspective from which to view the taxonomy. Thought of in this way, we can use it to pose questions based on whether we think students will benefit from a more concrete or abstract engagement with the lesson content.

For example, we might spend some time talking to a student who is struggling with the work. From our discussion we identify that their ability to think about the content in any abstract manner is severely hampered by their lack of certainty over the meaning of a series of key concepts. This leads us to conclude that questioning of a concrete order would be most beneficial in helping them to further their understanding.

I do not attempt to suggest that this is hugely different from the earlier point regarding the application of the taxonomy. It is simply a different way in which to think about the framework and the way in which we can apply it.

Some teachers find thinking about a continuum running from concrete to abstract a more useful approach. Often, they argue that this better reflects the reality of student knowledge and understanding. I include the approach here to offer you a different means by which to employ the taxonomy, should you wish to use it.

Chapter Nine – Assessment

Assessment is our penultimate focus. We will think about applying the taxonomy to support the twin aims of assessment: to sum up where students are at and to provide the information they need to make progress. These aims tally with the two types of assessment with which we are familiar: summative and formative. The first comes in the form of grades, marks or levels while the second comes in the form of verbal or written comments. The first is quantitative while the second is qualitative.

Assessment Overview

All assessment is contrived. This is as true for the twelve labours of Hercules as it is for next year's GCSE exams. The extent of the contrivance varies depending on what is being assessed, but the fact it is a contrivance remains true regardless.

This is not problem. The term is not used in a pejorative sense. The intention is to draw attention to the fact that all assessments are developed with some end in mind and do not arise naturally. By this I mean to contrast them to the content of the curriculum, which we might argue does arise naturally (for want of a better word) out of human thought and experience.

To put this another way, what we teach reflects a small amount of the sum of human knowledge and understanding. How we assess the extent to which students have grasped this is by contriving suitable questions or tasks which allow us to see the things for which we are looking; which give us access to the information we want to elicit.

If all assessment is contrived, it follows that the quality of the contrivance can vary. Assessments can be better or worse depending on their structure and on the thought which has gone into their development.

That this is the case can be seen by the frustration periodically witnessed when an exam board sets a paper which teachers and students feel runs contrary to the expectations engendered by the syllabus.

When constructing our own assessments, or working with those created by others, we need to pay attention to the quality of what we are creating or what is on offer. A few key points should be borne in mind when engaging in such analysis. Namely:

- Does the assessment fit with the relevant content?

- Will the assessment give rise to information which allows us to accurately judge the knowledge and understanding of our students?

- Is the assessment accessible for students, giving them scope through which to demonstrate their knowledge and understanding?

- Is the assessment sufficiently challenging to differentiate between varying levels of competency?

Considering these questions when constructing an assessment or when analysing one someone else has created means assessing the quality of the contrivance with which we aim to judge student knowledge and understanding. In the first case, this can lead us to adapt or amend the assessment we have developed. In the second case, it can lead us to decide whether or not what we have in front of us is fit for purpose.

As we will see in what follows, Bloom's Taxonomy is a uniquely powerful tool we can use when planning assessments. It is also one many other education professionals – including those who work for exam boards – call on when constructing their assessment.

General Points

The taxonomy is progressive. Successive levels are more challenging. Climbing the levels means gaining an increasing degree of mastery over the content with which we are concerned. It follows that the taxonomy provides a general framework for assessment.

We can use it to structure the questions or tasks we set students – whether these are formal assessments such as written tests in exam conditions, or informal assessments such as in-class tasks which we take in and mark.

We can also use the taxonomy as the basis of questioning, as per the last chapter. Verbal questioning is a type of informal assessment. It is the most common form of assessment which teachers do. Whenever we ask a question, we gain information about what students know and think. Using the taxonomy to frame our questioning helps elicit the kind of information we need to successfully assess student knowledge and understanding.

To create a formal or informal assessment which allows for sufficient discrimination between the relative ability levels of students, the taxonomy is a perfect tool. It gives us six separate points on which we can assess students. These can be thought of in isolation or they can be used in conjunction. However we approach their application, the purpose is the same: to develop assessments which make a range of cognitive demands on students, thus giving us the chance to elicit different kinds of information.

For example, most exam papers will contain a range of questions which get progressively more challenging. These often start at the lower levels of the taxonomy and move up towards the higher ones. Students who sit the exams all answer the same questions. Some do this more successfully than others. This results in exam scripts containing different information. By comparing this information to the mark-scheme, discrimination between candidates is achieved. So it is, for example, that Student A scores 55%, with most of their marks gained in the earlier questions based on knowledge, comprehension and application, while Student B scores 92%, gaining marks in the same areas as Student A, but also in the later areas predicated on analysis, synthesis and evaluation.

From this example we can see that many assessments, particularly formal ones, are tests of mastery. Students are judged against a set of criteria which determine the extent to which cognitive ability in a particular context has been demonstrated. The more answers they get right, the greater mastery they have exhibited if, and only if, the taxonomy is the framework underpinning the questions.

A couple of important points follow. First, assessments will ideally cover the taxonomy as a whole, giving students the chance to pick up marks for displaying effective cognition in relation to the different levels. Second, the weighting of the marks needs to reflect the desire for discrimination – and the range of that discrimination.

If a high proportion of marks are given for knowledge and comprehension, while only a small proportion are allotted to evaluation and synthesis, discrimination between students is difficult. Those who are more-able will not have the opportunity to be rewarded for their greater level of mastery.

Similarly, if the situation is reversed and only a few marks are given for knowledge and comprehension while the majority are given for evaluation and synthesis, students who are less-able will struggle to achieve any reward for the limited mastery they have developed.

It is for this reason that many exam boards define a series of Bloom's-based assessment objectives and then spread marks for each of these through their exam papers, with the balance tending to shift from the simpler objectives to the more complex ones as the paper progresses.

As an aside, these points highlight the inherent tension in summative assessment, played out in the argument over 'falling standards' and 'grade inflation.'

In-Lesson Assessment

We move now to practical strategies you can employ to assess students' knowledge and understanding. Here are three ways you can effectively conduct in-lesson assessment using Bloom's Taxonomy:

- Use mid-lesson review activities in which you take students through two or three levels of the taxonomy. This allows you to ascertain the extent to which they have understood the lesson content. You can then use this information to adapt the remainder of the lesson so that it best fits with where students are at.

For example, in a lesson looking at persuasive writing, we might introduce a mid-lesson review where we ask students to recall the key points of the lesson so far, explain these to a partner and then provide two examples of how they could be applied. This sees us assessing students' knowledge, comprehension and application.

The information we get as a result of this assessment is vital in helping us shape what we do next. We might find, say, that the class as a whole are expert in applying certain techniques we have looked at, but that when it comes to the other techniques the general level of mastery is rather more uneven. We could then revisit these techniques in the second half of the lesson to resolve the problem.

- Plan plenary activities which give students the chance to revisit and reinforce their learning but which also give you the opportunity to elicit useful information concerning mastery. For example, you might design a two-part plenary involving comprehension and synthesis. This would allow you elicit information about students' concrete and abstract understanding of the lesson content. Information you could then use to inform your future planning, making it more effective in the process.

- Devise mini-assessments which act as gateways between activities. This gives you the opportunity to assess mastery before you attempt to move the whole class from one task to the next. For example, you might ask a series of comprehension questions after the first activity, pose an analytical hinge question based on a common misconception after the second activity, and then ask for an evaluative summary in between the third activity and the plenary.

The benefit of this approach is twofold. First, you elicit information you can use to adapt and modify the lesson. Second, depending on the information you elicit, you can make the decision to move the learning onto the next activity, to slow things down and revisit what you have just done, or, you can split the class in half, move one group onto the next activity and spend time working with the other group to get them up to speed.

Question-Led Assessment

There are three main ways our assessments can be led: by question, by task or by product. We will look at each in turn, staring with the first.

Questioning has been covered in detail in the previous chapter. All that remains is to draw your attention to a few points regarding using questions as the basis of your assessments.

1. When using questions, it is important to consider what information these are likely to elicit. Closed questions will provide you with less information than open ones. However, this may be more specific and is a good way to check recall.

Higher-order questions, based on the top levels of the taxonomy, may require decoding. If you do not show students how to do this, they may struggle to answer them, or may answer them in a way which is different to what you want. It is helpful to teach students how to decode the command words connected to analysis, synthesis and evaluation. This gives them the tools through which to unlock more challenging questions.

2. Written questions can be supported by a series of bullet points indicating the areas at which students should look in their responses. Such an approach can be seen in a wide variety of GCSE question papers.

Here, the aim is to provide a breakdown of a complex question, scaffolding student responses by intimating what structure these should follow. When it comes to the taxonomy, we might set a complex question through which to test students' mastery at different levels and then break this down into three bullet points, the first of which looks at comprehension, the second at analysis and the third at evaluation.

Some argue this approach makes life too easy for students, removing the need to unpack questions. Others suggest that providing a scaffold means students have a better chance to demonstrate what they know and understand, and that doing this removes potentially unhelpful ambiguity over what is expected. I leave it to you to decide whether you want to employ this approach or not.

3. As we noted in Chapters Three, Four and Five each level of the taxonomy can be subdivided into different cognitive processes which, while retaining a core similarity, are subtly different. Hence evaluation covers assess, judge, rank and critique, four processes which all rest on a similar mental operation, but which are sufficiently different to require different words to signify them.

An interesting consequence of this is that, when planning question-led assessments, you might want to provide students with a selection of questions connected to any one level of the taxonomy, from which they then select the one (or two, or three) they would like to answer. This is similar to the situation we find in many exam-board assessments, where students have to choose from a set of similar questions.

The advantage of this approach is that it presents students with different opportunities through which to demonstrate their mastery.

Task-Based Assessment

In task-based assessment we take as our starting point the task we want students to complete. This could be the completion of a project, the answering of a set of questions or the demonstration of understanding in the context of a specific process. Tasks overlap with questions and products – in many cases, the assessments we develop will encompass all three. However, thinking about each separately affords a little clarity which might otherwise be hard to gain. To that end, here are three points to consider when developing task-based assessments:

- Consider the extent to which your tasks allows students the opportunity to show the various degrees of mastery they have gained over the content. This takes us back to our earlier point about whether an assessment has enough scope to sufficiently discriminate between different ability levels.

To ensure the tasks you set are broad enough in range, sit down and think about the competing responses a more-able and less-able student would be able to create given the demands the task makes. With these thoughts in mind you can enact a comparison before coming to a judgement about whether there is sufficient scope. If there is, the different responses will be far enough removed from one another to demonstrate very different degrees of mastery. If there isn't, the responses will be too close for the assessment to be as useful as you would like.

- A common means through which to structure task-based assessment is to state the overall task and to then provide a series of success criteria which help students to understand the different things they need to do to be successful.

You can tie these success criteria to different levels of the taxonomy. This means that, as students achieve each one, so too do they move up the taxonomy, demonstrating their relative mastery at each stage.

This helps you to elicit a wide range of information about student knowledge and understanding. It also ensures your assessment is differentiated. This is because different students are challenged by different success criteria. So, for example, one student might race through the first four before having to work hard to achieve number five, while another student might spend the whole task labouring to achieve numbers one, two and three.

- The simplest way to use the taxonomy to construct task-based assessments is to refer to the word lists first outlined in Chapter Two. Scan the lists, select a word which fits with the kind of assessment you want to create, and form a task accordingly.

For example, we might turn to the analysis list to construct an assessment at the end of a unit of work on the Vikings:

Analyse, Appraise, Categorize, Compare, Contrast, Differentiate, Discriminate, Distinguish, Examine, Experiment, Explore, Investigate, Question, Research, Test.

Scanning the list we decide that compare and contrast represent the key areas of analysis about which we want to know. From here we start to think about a task and perhaps settle on: Create a guide comparing and contrasting Viking life to the lives we lead today.

We see the inevitable intertwining of product and task here, as mentioned earlier. Nonetheless, in constructing this assessment, the task has been the focal point. The next step is to define success criteria and provide students with guidance covering the different areas of Viking life about which we want to know.

Product-Based Assessment

Third and finally we come to product-based assessment. In this context, we find ourselves developing assessments from the point of view of the products we want students to create. This may lead us to frame the assessment with a question – or to build it up out of a series of questions. Alternatively, it may cause us to ask students to do certain tasks. But, with this aside, by having the products we want students to create as our focus, different benefits can be occasioned compared to the other two approaches outlined above.

Here are three of the most important benefits which follow from working in this way:

- If the subject we are teaching involves a large practical element, then students will be best placed to demonstrate mastery by creating products of a certain type. This is typically true in subjects such as Art, Design and Technology and PE, as well as, to a lesser extent, Science and Maths.

In these situations, it makes sense to begin with the product and work from there. In so doing, we reinforce the primacy of the practical element and also find ourselves in a position from which we can structure the creation of the product so that students are encouraged to call on a variety of cognitive processes. By doing this, we give them every chance to display to us the mastery they have developed in terms of their knowledge and understanding.

- If the formal assessment point to which we are working requires students to create a product of a certain type, it make sense to mirror this in the prior assessments we develop. So, for example, if we are teaching History A Level and essay writing forms the basis of the exams students sit at the end of the course, we can start from the premise that our in-class assessments ought often to be essays.

Many teachers work in this way. It is an obvious path to follow. The benefits which accrue can be intensified by applying the different levels of the taxonomy to the product in question. Continuing our example, we might provide students with a guidance sheet or self-assessment pro-forma outlining what they need to do to demonstrate understanding, effective analysis and skilled evaluation during the course of their essays.

This helps students to write better pieces of work, more closely tied to the success criteria and the demonstration of mastery, than would otherwise be the case. The point can be applied in the context of nearly any product.

- Different products make different cognitive demands. This is a result of their structure which, in turn, infers what students need to focus on if they are to create a product of this type.

Essay-writing calls on different processes to report-writing. While there is overlap, there are also areas of exclusivity. This means the product on which you base your assessments will, in large part, define the type of cognitive processes students employ. Two points follow.

First, over time, it is helpful to vary the products students produce for assessment purposes. This gives an insight into different areas of their knowledge and understanding. Second, different areas of the curriculum may be better suited to certain types of products. In these cases, it would seem somewhat perverse to eschew such products. So doing will diminish the efficacy of our assessments, causing us to gain less information – and less useful information – than would otherwise be the case.

Constructing Mark-Schemes

Having developed an assessment with which to test the extent of our students' mastery, we now need to construct a mark-scheme to complete the circle. This is the set of criteria against which we judge the work students produce. This process allows us to ascertain how masterful students' thinking is, as well as what they need to do to develop further. In addition, we may decide to have students use the mark-scheme – either while they are working on their assessments or while they are engaged in peer- or self-assessment.

A number of options present themselves, each of which uses the taxonomy in a different way.

1. We can begin by defining what mastery looks like. This can happen in one of two ways. Either we imagine what it will look like, in which case we develop a clear sense of this in our mind's eye, or we use something

external – such as an exemplary piece of work – as the basis of our definition.

Whichever route we select, the next step is to break this definition down into a series of separate elements. These will roughly reflect the levels of the taxonomy. We will ask ourselves something along the lines of: 'What does the student need to do first, in terms of their knowledge? Then, how will they build on this to show understanding?'

Through this method, we find ourselves with a clearly defined endpoint which represents the pinnacle of the mark-scheme, as well as a series of steps, probably reflective of the taxonomy, which represent the separate elements of the mark-scheme; those bits which come before and beneath the creation of the final, masterful product.

Armed with this information we can quickly and effectively flesh out our skeleton, giving clear guidance as to what students need to do at each level to gain full marks and, overall, demonstrate mastery of the topic.

2. Take the taxonomy and use the six levels as the basis for six separate sections of your mark-scheme. Order these in accordance with the sequencing of the taxonomy, so as to maintain the gradual movement towards mastery.

This provides you with a general mark-scheme which can act as a starting point for something more precise. The next step is to begin at the level of knowledge and to carefully specify what students will need to be able to recall in order to gain full marks. Then, move on to comprehension and do the same. Repeat this until you have passed through all the levels.

The result will be a set of criteria closely modelled on the taxonomy but illustrated with specific examples at each stage. The process of going through and specifying the necessary content helps you to gain a clear sense of what you are looking for, making it easier for you to communicate this to your students.

3. An alternative to starting with the six levels is to opt for the three pairings we considered in Chapters Three, Four and Five. These are:

Knowledge and Comprehension

Application and Analysis

Synthesis and Evaluation

If you feel a six-level mark-scheme may be too cumbersome, this is an excellent alternative. Instead of seeing each level of cognitive processing as separate and distinct, we acknowledge, to some extent, the interwoven nature of thought and bundle together neighbouring levels accordingly.

This leaves us with a smaller mark-scheme. We have three general strands, each more demanding than the last. From here we can follow the same process as outlined above, fleshing out the framework with specific examples relevant to the curriculum. This quickly leads to a mark-scheme through which mastery can be effectively and efficiently judged.

The only caveat here is that, although we have gained a greater degree of simplicity by reducing the number of levels, this does mean the levels which remain are slightly more complex (because they combine separate processes). Furnishing them with specific examples is therefore slightly more demanding. This is by no means a major issue, but to be forewarned is to be forearmed.

4. Exemplar work is often an extremely helpful model for students. It provides an unambiguous sense of what success looks like, contextualising abstract ideas in a concrete form. Students can look at the work, analyse it, compare what they see to what they think the assessment is asking of them, and imitate or copy ideas they identify, with this being the starting point of successfully creating their own work.

You can build an effective mark-scheme by starting with exemplar work. Instead of simply defining what mastery looks like (as in point one, above), sit down and create mastery! That is, create a piece of exemplar work which, from your perspective, represents a masterful meeting of the demands your assessment makes.

You can use what you create as a model for students. You can also use it as the starting point of your mark-scheme. Simply work back from what you have created and identify the different elements which constitute your finished piece of work. Apply the taxonomy as you go to successfully draw out the different processes on which your work rests.

In this instance, the majority of your time will be taken up with creating the exemplar work. Analysing will not take long. This is because, through the process of making the exemplar, you will already have done much of the thinking necessary to define what success looks like.

5. Our final option is the simplest of the lot. If teaching an exam course, copy the mark-schemes provided by the exam board. As we have noted, these are invariably based on the taxonomy and, while you may want to adapt them to suit the assessments you create, the likelihood is that you will not want to deviate too much from what they set out as to do so could result in students developing a false sense of what success looks like.

You can use an exam board's mark-scheme in two different ways. First, you can copy it verbatim, constructing your assessment so it mirrors the style of assessment in the final exams. In this case all you need do is swap the content contained in the mark-scheme so it matches what your assessment is about.

Second, apply the mark-scheme by using its structure and general principles but modify these so they fit with the particular assessment you have constructed. This approach gives you a little more leeway but is also more time-consuming.

Chapter Ten – Stretch and Challenge

We conclude our examination of Bloom's Taxonomy and how to use it in the classroom by turning to stretch and challenge. Up to this point, we have thought about these ideas in general terms. Throughout, we have indicated how using the taxonomy to underpin planning, shape activities and inform questioning can help you to push students' thinking and raise achievement. In this chapter we will examine specific strategies, activities and techniques through which you can do this.

What follows can be used to stretch and challenge your more-able students or as a means through which to stretch and challenge all students. The balance you seek to draw will depend on the students you teach and the wider intentions you have for your teaching. Suffice to say, everything outlined can be adapted and applied for either scenario.

Challenge as a Supplement

To begin, let us recast challenge so we might look at it in two ways. First, challenge is an integral part of any lesson, permeating our planning and teaching. Second, challenge is a supplement to the lesson – something we add on; an extra element designed to take thinking and learning further than would otherwise be the case.

In the rest of the book, we focussed on challenge in the first sense. We looked at the taxonomy as a route to mastery, considering how to apply it to our lesson planning and how to adapt it for use in activities and questioning.

In this chapter, we focus on the second sense; challenge as a supplement. We look at ways in which we can use the taxonomy to add more to our already challenging lessons. The additions we make are aimed primarily at stretching and challenging the thinking of our more-able students.

However, they will also be open to all students. Keeping challenge supplements exclusive diminishes the potential scope of their application. While we do not assume all students will get onto and complete all the supplements we plan, the point is to retain in our minds the idea that, while they are aimed predominantly at our more-able students, every student can potentially benefit from them as well.

For example, we might plan extension activities which our more-able students tend to access on a regular basis. In addition though, we might also use these as a point of challenge with which to push our middle-ability students. This could see us circulating during the course of the main activity, drawing those students' attention to the extension tasks and challenging them to aim for these, even if they had not previously considered such an aim particularly likely.

Operating in this way means we turn challenge supplements into a tool for pushing all students, encouraging them to work harder and think further than might otherwise have been the case.

Another point to note is that, although the supplements are outlined as if designed for use with more-able students, there is nothing to stop you adapting and modifying them for use with other students. This might even involve creating two or three separate challenge supplements, with each one aimed at a different group in the class.

In short, the ideas which follow help you to apply the taxonomy to stretch and challenge the thinking of your most-able students. You can adapt and modify them to challenge the rest of your class as well. The choice is yours!

Extension Tasks and Questions

Extension tasks and questions represent additional work appended to whole-class activities. Outstanding lessons are likely to have these at every stage – from the starter through to the plenary. This means throughout the lesson, every student in the class knows there is more challenging work waiting for them, should they get onto it.

A potential pitfall is the creation of extension tasks and questions which are seen by students as simply more of the same. This can be demotivating. Students feel the challenge is to repeat what has already been done, only in a slightly different way or with slightly different content.

Avoiding this situation is important because challenge tasks should be fun and engaging. After all, we are looking to promote a love of learning and that, undoubtedly, ought to include a love of having your thinking challenged and, through this, pushed to new heights.

Three simple techniques present themselves, all involving use of the taxonomy:

- First, we can create extension questions using a different level of the taxonomy from that which underpins the main activity. For example, we might plan a main activity based mostly on analysis and supplement this with an evaluation-based extension question. This ensures the challenge is rooted in a different cognitive process and does not just ask students to do more of the same.

- Second, if your activity is already at the top of the taxonomy in terms of the work it is asking students to do, you can plan an extension calling on a different level which is similarly challenge. This harks back to the point we made earlier about synthesis and evaluation being interchangeable. So, if you have a main activity predicated on evaluation, plan a supplement based on synthesis, and vice versa.

- Third, if neither of the previous two options are possible, return to the taxonomy keyword lists and identify a keyword which is sufficiently different from that driving the main task to warrant inclusion as the basis of an extension. For example, if your main task is concerned with evaluation in the form of 'assessment,' you could devise an extension based around 'defend' or 'rank.' While this technique does not give rise to the same level of difference as the previous two, it still serves to create enough difference for students not to feel they are just being asked to do more of the same.

Project Work

Project work is where we give students an independent task to complete as they see fit, usually over an extended period. As a challenge supplement, this involves giving students a project to which they can return, every time they complete the main activity we have set for the whole class.

For example, we might set our most-able Year 6 students a project in which they have to produce a detailed guide to a topic of their choosing, with this caveated by a series of success criteria designed to keep them focussed on producing high-quality work.

In this situation, our most-able students will return to their project work whenever they finish a main activity, stretching their thinking as a result. Over time, they will produce an extended piece of work which reflects their interest in whichever topic they have chosen.

The key features of project work are that it is open-ended, independent and, generally, thematic. Because it requires students to think at length and in depth about a particular topic or area, it necessarily promotes analytical, creative and critical thinking, placing it in line with the top three levels of the taxonomy. In addition, if we give such work to our most-able students, leaving them free to make choices about what they study and how they study this, they will be naturally inclined to engage with information and ideas at a reasonably high level.

This is for two reasons. First, the independent and open-ended nature of project work is motivating. If students are motivated they are more likely to push the limits of their thinking and pursue what they are doing to a point of challenge. Second, the project will come to lack meaning for the students in question if the thinking they do remains at too concrete a level. This may be a starting point, but they will have to push beyond it if they really want to grasp hold of the material. Having been given choice and ownership over the project, it is likely students will want to do this.

When providing success criteria to structure project work, it is always worth referring to the taxonomy. This means you can ensure students are directed to think increasingly deeply about the material in question.

A simple approach is to provide five success criteria, basing these respectively on comprehension, application, analysis, synthesis and evaluation. Another option is to go for three success criteria (which some students find more manageable) and to base these on some combination of the five categories mentioned (while maintaining a bias towards the higher levels).

A final point to note is that much project work is inherently creative. This is because it sets students a general task and asks them to choose how best to meet this challenge. As we know, creative thinking is near the top of the taxonomy, in the form of synthesis. Hence, we have another reason as to why project work stretches and challenges students' thinking.

Creative Independence

Let us stay on this theme of creativity by turning to the general idea of creative independence. This, we might say, characterises people such as artists, musicians, scientists and writers, among others, who are at the top of their field. It reflects the fact that these individuals have reached a point from which development has become their own end to shape. They have achieved mastery and moved beyond it.

Consider, for example, an artist such as Henri Matisse. His fame and regard stems not just from his mastery of technique, but so too from the manner in which he took that mastery and used it to explore and develop new avenues of form and representation.

Creative independence is thus highly valued in our society, as well as being highly challenging.

We can create supplements to our lessons through which to encourage creative independence in our most-able students. Here are three approaches:

- Use the synthesis keywords to construct tasks or questions which give students scope to be creative on their own terms. This is a step beyond the project work and extension tasks outlined above. Here, our aim is to deliberately foster a sense of freedom and lack of structure (whereas in those two examples our aim was to foster freedom *with* a structure). For example, we might ask students to create, design or plan something new. Or we might ask them to try to solve a problem, suggest an alternative, or sketch a different way of doing something.

- Challenge students to engage creatively with the lesson content but to do so with the intention of failing. This takes us back to the idea of trial and error along with the feedback loop which comes from continued failure and analysis. To do this, you should again look to the synthesis keywords as a starting point for constructing tasks or questions. Beyond this, however, you should also explain to students that success will not be measured by the finished products they create, but by the number of failures they come up with and what they learn from each one. We are turning student expectations upside down so as to encourage a new, more challenging way of thinking. One which is based on creative independence.

- Remove the shackles. During whole-class activities, work with your more-able students to quickly assess that they have grasped the main ideas, then give them the freedom to take the learning in a direction which interests them. Do this by engaging in a brief, speculative discussion about what the ideas or information might mean, lead to or how they might connect to other areas of knowledge. Encourage students to come to some form of conclusion through the discussion – a question, task or problem which can animate their thinking – and then leave them to pursue this under their own steam.

Critical and Creative Thinking Skills

We can directly improve the critical and creative thinking skills of our students by providing challenge supplements which focus on these. An obvious approach is to use tailored questions (as outlined in Chapter Eight) based on the top three levels of the taxonomy. Here are four more ideas you might also like to try:

- Challenge students to make and explain connections between the lesson content and other areas of the syllabus, including areas which might, at first glance, have little to connect them to the current topic. Making connections involves lateral thinking, which is inherently creative.

You can scaffold this type of thinking by giving students a model of how to make connections. You might demonstrate, for example, how we can look for similarities of type or category, such as when we note a connection between a historical interpretation and a design solution. Both fall into the category of creative thinking whereby we take what is known and use our skills to turn it into something new which solves the problem we faced.

- Provide students with a set of critical questions they can apply in various situations, no matter the information and ideas with which they are presented. The nature of these questions will differ depending on your subject, but the emphasis is on coming up with a set of 3-5 which you can challenge students to consistently apply. So doing will help them to develop their critical thinking as they come to internalise the questions along with the ways of thinking they promote.

- Challenge students to speculate using the question stem 'What if...' This is another example of synthesis-led questioning. Here the focus is on developing plausible responses to the conditional hypothesis indicated by the question stem. You can control the extent to which you structure student thinking by altering the degree of emphasis you place on providing evidence-backed justification for any speculations. The higher you set the bar for evidence, the more control you exert over the creative thinking students do.

- While students are engaged in a task, circulate through the room and give more-able students a target through which to assess the work they have done so far. This target could be in the form of a question (What could you do to make your work more accurate?) or a statement (Look at your use of rhetorical techniques and assess the impact it is going to have on the reader). Either way, the aim is to help students view their own work critically by giving them a focus for real-time self-assessment. Increase the efficacy of the approach by returning to students a few minutes later to discuss with them what they have uncovered.

Creative Trial and Error

We mentioned creative trial and error earlier when we thought about creative independence. Now we will look at the idea in more depth, examining different ways through which you can encourage more-able students to embrace the approach.

Creative trial and error involves trying things out, making mistakes, and then reviewing the information elicited by those mistakes. This information covers what happened, what went wrong, how this relates to what was attempted, and what the consequences are for trying again.

When we talk about information, we are talking about that immediately elicited (and visible or knowable through observation or experience of the failure) as well as that elicited through subsequent analysis and reflection. Both types are important. One without the other leads to less successful creative development.

Here are three ways you can challenge students to engage in creative trial and error:

- Challenge more-able students to take on harder problems. These could be more complex, require a higher degree of knowledge and understanding, or be set just beyond the boundary of what students are currently capable of. In each case, creative trial and error is required to try to solve the problems; or, at least, to get closer to solving them.

You should encourage students to see the process – that of trialling ideas and assessing the results – as more important than the end to which they are aiming (solving the problem). This is because the process can be developed and applied in other settings, and because it is the process which reveals information about the nature of the problem and the current extent of students' knowledge and understanding. It is the process which leads to learning, rather than the endpoint of effectively solving the problem.

- Give students a different starting point compared to what they are used to and challenge them to pursue a task or question from there. For example, a more-able student may have honed a fairly sound technique for answering essay questions. Let us imagine they come up with a paragraph plan, note this down and then set about implementing it.

At the start of an essay-writing activity you would go up to them and present a different starting point which they have to trial. For example, you might tell them they need to write their conclusion first, then their last paragraph, then their penultimate paragraph and so on, until they reach the introduction. This will be hard for them! They will have to think more deeply than they are used to. Creative trial and error will be heavily involved. As a result, they will gain a better understanding of the process of essay writing and how to apply their knowledge to the construction of a final piece of work. They may well return to their original technique in subsequent tasks, but this will be enhanced by the information elicited during the process of creative trial and error.

- When students have completed a piece of work, ask them to go back through it and identify three alternative decisions they could have made. This works better with a fairly large piece of work. In smaller pieces, it is unlikely there will be enough content for students to pick out sufficient alternative decision points.

When students have their points, challenge them to choose one and to redo that section of their work based on a different choice they could have made. This involves them trialling a previously rejected option and judging the results of this.

A great benefit of such an approach is that it gives students an analytical insight into the process of creation. Going back and examining the decisions taken to produce a piece of work involves looking closely at the process of creation – much more closely than you might normally do. This yields information otherwise inaccessible; as does the subsequent task of redoing a section of work based on an alternative decision. Overall, the technique helps students better understand how to successfully create products and gives them an idea of how making different choices can lead to radically different results.

Regular Evaluation: Expecting Justification

As part of your efforts to stretch and challenge students' thinking, you should aim to include evaluation in your lessons on a regular basis. Doing so means you will always be encouraging students to hit the top level of the taxonomy.

Evaluation can be included in the form of extension questions and tasks, tailored questions, sub-tasks forming part of a main activity as well as through the objectives and outcomes you plan.

However, there is another technique we have at our disposal. One we can use as a supplement and which is easier to apply to the class as a whole than anything else mentioned in this chapter.

Put simply, we can always, always expect justification from our students when they share an answer to a question or make a claim.

Justification is the means through which we defend and support the things we assert. It is the main method of persuasion on which arguments rely. The dominant forms of justification are reason, evidence and example. Reason is the attempt to logically prove a point in relation to given premises. Evidence is where we call on things extant or known to support our assertions. Examples can be abstract or concrete demonstrations of what we are asserting. Sometimes they overlap with evidence, sometimes they don't.

You can communicate that you expect justification by always calling on students to provide reasons, evidence and/or examples to support what they say. You can do this when students answer questions, when you engage them in discussion and when you mark their work. In each situation, you will be making it clear that an answer or response only meets your standards if it comes with sufficient justification.

To help students achieve this, you should provide clear models of what justification looks like – including specific examples pertaining to each of the three key areas: reason, evidence and examples.

In terms of using the technique to challenge your most-able students, you can expect more justification from them than from other students. You can also expect their justifications to be more detailed and more nuanced. So, for example, you might discuss a problem with one of your more-able students during the course of an activity and then press them to fully justify the answer the solution they suggest. As part of this, you might choose to hone in on one of the three areas – evidence, say – to focus their minds more precisely.

Another option is to set additional success criteria for your more-able students connected to the level of justification you expect them to provide, either verbally or in writing, depending on the nature of the task. These can be general, or they can be similar to that outlined in the last paragraph, with specific reference being made to one of the three types of justification.

Consistently pushing your students to provide more detailed or more nuanced justification than they would otherwise posit sees them quickly developing a more critical engagement with the topics you teach. You can further develop their skills by drawing attention to the process in which you are engaged. Through this you can highlight what justification involves and why it is always to be welcomed. This helps increase the extent of students' metacognition – the thinking they do about the thinking you ask them to do(!).

Refining Judgements

This is a development of the previous point, yet a technique sufficiently different to warrant a separate entry. Consider the following judgements:

- Goldilocks should be given a certain degree of leeway because it is difficult to resist porridge when you are very hungry.

- Goldilocks should be given a certain degree of leeway because it is difficult to resist porridge when you are very hungry. However, the leeway should be limited because Goldilocks needs to understand the boundaries of acceptable behaviour. If she does not, she is likely to face more serious consequences in the future.

The second judgement is more refined than the first. By refined we mean that it has been thought through in greater detail. This leads to a more developed final product.

If we refine something, we improve it, purify it or do both. In terms of judgements, those that have been refined rest on greater prior engagement with that being judged. A student who presents you with a refined judgement has done more intellectual work than one who gives you an unrefined judgement.

So how does this play out as a classroom technique?

We can indicate to more-able students that we do not expect them to present judgements – either verbally or in writing – that are unrefined. To help them meet our expectations, we can provide a set of exemplar questions or a thinking model to apply whenever they make a judgement. By repeatedly using this, they will soon refine the quality of their thinking.

So, for example, we might give more-able students in our A Level Sociology class the following set of questions to apply:

- What does my judgement assume and should it assume this?

- Is my judgement too broad? Am I making claims larger than I can justify?

- Does my judgement take into account arguments with which I disagree? If not, should it?

These questions will help our students to make more refined judgements. If they use them repeatedly – every time they assess a sociological idea, theory or study – they will be continuously improving their ability to evaluate. Over time, we might replace the questions with more challenging ones – or invite students to suggest their own.

As ever, you can apply the idea across the board. Simply adapt the questions or model you provide to fit the age-group and/or subject you are teaching.

Defending Unfavourable Positions

We all tend to make judgements which accord with our more deeply held positions. This is not always the case as, for example, when we attempt to remain disinterested during the passing of judgement (and, in fact, one definition of good judgement is that we judge each case on its merits, avoiding the temptation to let our proclivities bias our perspective). However, it is true that for all of us – students included – connecting judgements to our own biases is a common habit.

The corollary of this fact is that defending unfavourable positions – positions with which we disagree, or for which we cannot see a great deal of evidence – is challenging. Here are five ways you can use this point to stretch students' thinking:

- When a more-able student completes a piece of work containing an assessment, read through what they have done and challenge them to effectively justify a contrary position.

- Assign arguments at random to more-able students in your class and insist they develop a means through which to justify whatever has been assigned.

- Write down a series of unfavourable positions connected to the topic, each on a separate slip of paper. Fold these up and place them in a cup. Invite more-able students to select one at random. They then have to justify their selections.

- Ask more-able students to mount a defence of a position they don't agree with by thinking from the perspective of somebody else. For example, if a student doesn't believe that fossil fuels should be used indiscriminately, ask them to consider how an executive working for a multinational oil company might argue against this.

- Challenge students to argue something they know to be untrue. For example, you might ask students to argue that black is in fact white, or that Little Red Riding Hood did not actually get eaten by the Big Bad Wolf. Here, the exercise is about pure argumentation, rather than anything else.

And on that note we draw our discussion to a close noting, in summary, that using Bloom's Taxonomy to stretch and challenge students means, in general, developing supplements based on the higher levels, and then using these regularly as part of the lessons you teach. All that is left is for us to draw our wider discussion to a conclusion, which we will do next.

Conclusion

So there we have it, Bloom's Taxonomy in all its wonder: known, comprehended, applied, analysed, assessed and used as the basis of new ideas and techniques.

Personally, I am of the belief that the taxonomy is the most underrated tool in the teacher's armoury. As we have seen, it can be applied to a wide variety of areas, every time acting as a framework through which to raise achievement, stretch and challenge students' thinking and help them to move along the path to mastery.

It provides a brilliant foundation for lessons, activities, questioning, assessment, challenges, outcomes and objectives. It is adaptable and can be moulded to fit any area of the curriculum and almost any age-group.

The efficacy of the tool can be seen from its continued use – and central role in much of education – today, some half a century or more after its initial development.

Given as how the taxonomy reflects a largely unchanging structure of thought, it is my belief that its usefulness will remain high for decades to come. I hope that, through this book and the ideas contained therein, I have been able to convey to you my enthusiasm for the framework and provide you with many practical strategies you can employ in your own planning, teaching and assessment.

Finally, I wish you good luck in your endeavours and in your efforts to apply the taxonomy in your classroom, wherever you are and whatever you are teaching. I'm sure your students will benefit greatly as a result.

Select Bibliography

Anderson, Lorin W.; Krathwohl, David R., eds. (2001). *A taxonomy for learning, teaching, and assessing: A revision of Bloom's taxonomy of educational objectives*. Allyn and Bacon.

Bloom, B. S.; Engelhart, M. D.; Furst, E. J.; Hill, W. H.; Krathwohl, D. R. (1956). *Taxonomy of educational objectives: The classification of educational goals*. Handbook I: Cognitive domain. New York: David McKay Company.

Bloom, B. S. (1994). Rehage, Kenneth J.; Anderson, Lorin W.; Sosniak, Lauren A., eds. "Bloom's taxonomy: A forty-year retrospective". *Yearbook of the National Society for the Study of Education* (Chicago: National Society for the Study of Education) **93** (2).

Harrow, Anita J. (1972). *A taxonomy of the psychomotor domain: A guide for developing behavioral objectives*. New York: David McKay Company.

Krathwohl, D. R.; Bloom, B. S.; Masia, B. B. (1964). *Taxonomy of educational objectives: The classification of educational goals*. Handbook II: the affective domain. New York: David McKay Company.

Krathwohl, David R. (2002). "A revision of Bloom's taxonomy: An overview". *Theory Into Practice* (Routledge) **41** (4): 212–218.

Appendix 1 – Ready-to-use Comprehension Questions

Identify

How might an alien identify X?

What helps you to identify X?

What might you need to know to successfully identify X?

What might you need to know to identify specific types of X?

How could you be misled when trying to identify X?

What problems can you imagine for a novice attempting to identify X? How might they avoid or overcome these?

How might you identify X by looking at differences?

How might you decide which things X should go with?

What terms could you use to write about X?

How might it be possible for two strangers who have never met to both identify the same thing as X?

Imagine you were deprived of one/two/three/four senses. Which senses/combinations of senses might allow you to identify X? Why?

What might have to happen to make X unidentifiable?

Who could be most skilled at identifying X and why?

When and where might it be useful to know how to identify X?

Think back to when you couldn't identify X. What might a story of your learning since then be like? What dramas were there? Did failures takes place, or particular successes? What helped you become able to identify X?

What might have to happen for you to be better able to identify X in the future?

How might you break X down into a series of identifiable categories?

What features does X have that help you to identify it?

(Thus – How might the unique combination of these identify X?)

Can you identify the words/images/sounds which might link to X? Why do these things link?

If X was among a selection of similar things, how would you identify it?

How might identifying X be different in different situations?

Could two people identify two separate things as X? How? Why?

Think about the way you have decided X can be identified. How might someone critique this?

Is there a conclusive/definitive way of identifying X?

Is X's identity unique?

When and why might X's identity be subsumed by a broader group identity? (For example, when and why does an oak tree become part of a wood?)

Can you identify X from this list? How were you able to do that?

Express

How did X make you feel or think?

What feelings or thoughts did X bring forth in you? Why might this have happened?

What feelings or thoughts might other people express because of X? Why?

Does X make you feel and think different things, or are your feelings and thoughts connected? What are the reasons for this?

How might X have influenced your feelings or thoughts?

How could you use your body to express what X has made you think or feel?

How might you use colour/sound/shape/rhythm/touch to express that which X has made you think or feel?

What might someone think of X? Why?

What thoughts or feelings might person A and person B have about X? How and why might they differ?

How might you express your feelings about X?

What is your opinion of X?

How might you defend your opinion of X?

What reasons, examples or evidence might there be to support your opinion of X?

How might you express X in the context of Y?

How might you use Y as a means to express X?

Why might X lead someone to think or feel certain things?

If X changed, how might your thoughts and feelings about X change as well?

How might a change in Y affect your thoughts and feelings about X?

What might the world be like if no one was allowed to express their thoughts or feelings about X?

What might the world be like if everyone could read other people's thoughts and feelings about X?

How might people think or feel differently about X in different situations?

How could you show how X made you think or feel?

Is there anything which we cannot express ourselves about? If so, why is this? If not, can you think of a situation where we would not in fact be able to express ourselves?

How might you express your thoughts or feelings about X if you were deprived of one/two/three/four senses?

How much of an influence are other factors (for example, past experiences) on your thoughts and feelings about X? How might this be problematic or beneficial?

How might language help you to express your views on X?

How might language hinder you when expressing your views on X?

Where might you be best able to express your views on X? Why?

How might your initial thoughts or feelings about X change following reflection?

Describe

How might you describe X?

How might you describe X through actions/words/pictures?

What effect might context have on your description of X?

How might you describe X differently for different audiences? What might be the consequences of this? What might this tell you about the relationship between audience(s) and description?

How might you describe the changes in X over time period Y?

Can you describe how X changes over time?

Can you give a detailed description of X? What might you need to include for your description to be 'detailed'?

How might a description of X be different from a detailed description of X? What might be the consequences, intended or otherwise, of these differences?

How might person A describe X?

How might person A and person B differ in their descriptions of X? What might be the reasons for this?

What effect could motivation or desire Y have on a person's description of X?

Can you describe the constituent parts of X? How does this compare with a general description of X?

How might you describe X to someone deprived of sight/smell/touch/taste/hearing? How might the loss of sense Y affect your ability to describe X?

How might subjective and objective descriptions of X differ? Can *any* description of X be seen as truly objective?

What would you describe as the key features of X?

Can you describe how X makes you feel? Can you describe the connotations X has? Can you describe the associations with X that you have in your mind?

How might you describe the purpose/design/intention/effects/impact of X?

How might you describe the forces which influence X?

How might you describe the relationship X has to its surroundings?

How might a positive description of X differ from a critical description?

How might you describe X so as to take into account conflicting viewpoints?

Where might a description of X prove useful?

Why might it be necessary to describe X?

Who might benefit from a description of X? In what ways would they benefit?

In what circumstances might a description of X prove contentious/useful/vital/helpful/unwieldy? Why?

Before describing X, what criteria do you think would best underpin your description? Why?

How might you best communicate a description of X? Why would this be the best method?

Explain

How might you explain X?

How might you explain X person A or group B?

How might you explain X through writing/dance/drama/speaking/symbols?

What might person A need to know in order to explain X?

When might you need to be able to explain X?

When might an explanation of X come in useful? Why? What might this tell us about X?

Who might be able to explain X? Who might make use of an explanation of X? How might they use it?

How might interpreting X be different to explaining it? (And so on with a wide range of alternative verbs)

Why might X be as it is?

What can you tell us about the functions or purpose of X?

Can you explain why you think that?

Can you give a reason for that? What might be a reason for that?

How might you explain your reasoning/actions/behaviour/choices?

In what circumstances might it be necessary to explain X?

What might be the most effective way of explaining X (...in situation Y/ to person A)?

Considering what you already know, how might you try and explain 'new knowledge X'?

How might X affect your explanation?

New information X appears to contradict/challenge your explanation. How might you explain this problem? How might you alter your explanation to take account of it?

Why might there be different explanations of X? What can we gain/infer/deduce from this? How might these explanations be reconciled? How might the differences/similarities affect our own understanding of X?

How might explaining X help you to understand it?

How might X be explained by theory Y/person A?

How might the effects of X help to explain its purpose/meaning/role/behaviour?

Can you explain what happened? Why might it have happened?

How might you explain the connection between X and Y?

Of the explanations, whose do you find most acceptable? Why?

What might X help you to explain?

What criteria might you use to judge the different explanations of X?

How might you assess an explanation of X?

If you emphasise different factors, how might your explanation of X alter?

When explaining X, what effect might context have?

Translate

How might you show X through medium Y?

How might you express X using dance/drama/poetry/algebra?

Can you draw X?

Can you draw your understanding of X?

How might you explain X using different words?

How might you explain X in simpler terms?

How might individuals A and B explain X differently?

If today's learning was turned into a snappy chant, what might it sound like?

Having drawn together the key information, what might it be like as a Haiku?

How might you translate X into form Y?

How might you translate your learning for audience Y?

What might change about X if you were to translate it into medium Y?

What aspects of X will remain most visible if you translate it into medium Y? What does this tell us about X? What does it tell us about medium Y?

Who might find it necessary to translate X, or have it translated for them, in order to aid their understanding? Why?

What essential features of X might be highlighted if we translate it into medium Y?

Where and when might it be useful to translate X into a different form?

Why might translating X into a different form help your own understanding?

Why might translating X into a different form be difficult?

What process might you have to go through in order to translate X into medium/form Y?

How might you translate X using anything you have learnt in maths/science/French (or any other subject)?

What might an equation of your learning look like?

How might you translate X so that it made sense to an alien/animal/plant?

How would you know that a translation made sense? What assumptions would you have to make when translating the material? Why?

How might your understanding of X change when you translate it into medium/form Y? What might this tell us about X, our understanding, or the medium?

Imagine person A was deprived of sense Z. How might you translate X so they were able to understand it?

Imagine you met a group of people with who you could not communicate through language. How might you try to explain X to them?

How might you translate what you have learnt into a form appropriate for audience Y? What form might you choose and why do you think it is appropriate?

How might you explain X using gestures?

Appendix 2 – Ready-to-use Application Questions

Apply

How might you use X to deal with situation Y?

In what circumstances might X apply?

When/where might X apply?

What applications of X might there be?

How might two individuals apply X differently?

How might a change in context affect the application of X?

How might the motives or intentions of person A affect how they apply X?

How would you decide whether X can be applied in various situations?

How could you use X to solve problem Y?

If X changed, could it still be applied to Y/in situation Y?

How might group or person A use X to improve their situation?

How might you change X so as to alter its uses? What unintended consequences might your changes cause?

In which situations might you apply X rather than Y (and vice versa)?

Can you develop a rule/set of rules explaining when it is appropriate to use X?

How might you use X in your everyday life?

What uses of X might there be?

Imagine element Z of X was to change, how might this affect the uses of X?

To what extent can X be changed, yet its uses remain the same? What might this tell us about X? What might this tell us about the relationship between X's structure and its use?

What might be the implications of applying X to Y/situation Y?

Could X be applied in situations for which it was not originally intended/in which it is not traditionally used? What might be the results of this?

Why might it be possible to apply X to Y?

Can you construct a table outlining situations where you could apply X, and those where you could not apply it? From this, what conclusions might you be able to draw about X and its uses?

Might there be situations where X does not apply? Do these have something in common? If so, what might this tell us about X?

Imagine someone had not encountered X before. Can you provide guidance that would explain how, when, where and why to apply it?

How much do you need to know about X in order to use it successfully?

How might knowing more about X change how you use it?

Can you think of a situation where X was once useful, but is not anymore?

Sketch

Can you sketch X?

If you were to sketch X, what parts would you choose as most important?

What might a general outline of X look like?

How might you sketch different parts of X?

Can you sketch separate parts of X so as to suggest what the whole of X looks like?

What bits of X would a sketch miss out? Would it always be the same? Why?

How might the demands of the audience affect a sketch of X?

Imagine you were asked to include element Y in your sketch of X. How might this alter it? On reflection, what might this tell us about your original sketch?

How might person A and person B sketch X differently?

What might a sketch reveal about the sketcher's beliefs/feelings/thoughts about X? How would you test to see if this was true?

Imagine you had to sketch an outline of X. What would you choose as the most important things to include?

How might a brief account of X differ from a general outline?

What constraints might you come across when sketching an outline of X? How could you overcome these?

How might oral and written sketches of X differ?

Briefly, what is X and how does it work?

How would you ensure accuracy in a general outline of X?

Can you give a brief account of X and explain what parts you think are worthy of further consideration?

How might a sketch of X benefit us/an audience/yourself?

How might a sketch of cause difficulties for us/an audience/yourself?

How would you sketch the main features of X?

How might a brief written account of X and a brief oral account of X differ in emphasis or content?

When might a general outline of X prove most useful?

Why might a brief account of X be better than a full explanation?

How might we judge whether a general outline of X is true or not? Could some bits be true, yet the overall account false?

When dealing with sketches of X, what might we need to be mindful of (compared to when handling all the facts)?

How might a sketch of X lead to misconceptions? What might these misconceptions be? How could you make sure that a sketch of X was clear and accurate?

How might the brief accounts of X by individuals A,B and C be reconciled? Would we want to reconcile them? Why?

Choose

Which option could be best for person A? Why?

Which item/tool/concept/idea might best suit the task?

How might you go about choosing from selection X?

What criteria might you use to make a decision about X?

How might your choice(s) about X be different if you used different criteria?

What guidelines would you give someone to help them make choices in situation Y?

Which option might be best in situation Y? Why? How might a change in the situation affect this choice?

How might you approach project X in order to meet the success criteria?

What previous knowledge might be of most use to you here?

Based on theory N, what choices might you make in situations X,Y,Z?

Would you choose theory M or theory N to explain situations X,Y,Z? What are your reasons for your choices?

How might your choices be affected by motives/emotions/rationality/competing claims/morality/opportunity cost?

What might your choice lead you to forgo?

When might your choice be called into question?

If your choice was questioned, how would you explain it?

How might you defend your choice?

What might cause you to alter your choice?

What might be the best form of X in situation Y?

Which option might be most appropriate? Why? On what does this depend? How might change over time/in space/in thought/of people/of culture affect this decision?

What reasons might someone give for opposing your choice?

How might you explain your choice, and the reasons/method behind this, to someone not familiar with the situation/material?

How might the learning help us to choose between X and Y?

What reasoning might you apply to situation X in order to make a decision?

Why might individuals A and B make different choices in situation X?

How might two people use the same knowledge but come to different decisions?

How might you decide what to do in situation X?

What would give you the best opportunity to show your knowledge/skills/understanding?

How might we explain person A's choice in situation X?

Who might choose option X? Why?

Demonstrate

How might you demonstrate X?

How might you demonstrate your understanding of X?

How might you demonstrate your understanding of X in situation Y?

How might you demonstrate rule/theory/concept/idea X?

What might you need/need to know in order to demonstrate X?

Can you show me how to use X?

How might you demonstrate X through drama/miming/facial expressions/noises?

How might you try to demonstrate that X is right?

How might you show that X is true?

How might audience Y/context Z affect your ability to demonstrate X?

What features are demonstrated by X?

How might you demonstrate what you have learnt today?

Why/when/where might it be necessary to demonstrate an understanding of X?

How might you use today's learning?

How might you put what you have learnt to practical use?

If you were to be assessed, how might you demonstrate your knowledge/understanding?

What skills/knowledge could you demonstrate in situation X?

Imagine situation/relationship/idea X changed. How would you show that you understood the implications of this change?

Given Y, how might you demonstrate its effects on X?

What skills is person A demonstrating in situation/clip X? What does this information tell us?

What might the existence of X demonstrate?

What might the behaviour/work/speech of person A demonstrate?

Thinking about demonstrating X, how might you break the process down into separate parts? (For example: first unplug the kettle, then fill it with water, then plug it in and turn it on...etc.)

What might be the most effective way of demonstrating X? What are your reasons for this? How might it be affected by who the audience is? How might it be affected by the method/means of communication?

When demonstrating X, what might you expect person A to show/take account of/elucidate?

How much might person A have to demonstrate for you to judge what they are doing as good? Why?

Who might be most capable of demonstrating X? Why? How could you narrow the gap between that person's capabilities and your own? What might their abilities tell you about the nature of X?

How could you demonstrate the connection between X and Y?

Are there things you simply cannot demonstrate? If so, what are they and why can't you demonstrate them? If not, what might this tell us about humans and how they communicate?

Solve

How might you solve X?

How might person A try to solve X?

What might you use/need to solve X?

How might you use what we have learnt today to solve X?

How might Y help you to solve X?

What else might you require to solve X? How/why have you reached that conclusion?

How might we solve the problem? What might the ramifications of solving it be? How might they relate to the means by which it is solved?

What might be the answer to /explanation of X?

How might you go about trying to solve problem X? Why would you choose such a method? What alternatives are there? What might these offer which is different from your original idea?

What might explain X?

How might we best deal with X? Why might this be the best way?

What might you need in order to try and solve X?

Under what circumstances, or for who, might it be necessary to solve X? What might this tell us about the nature of X?

What motivation might an individual/group have for solving X?

How might you use reasoning to solve/explain X?

How might you have solved situation X? Would it have differed from what actually happened? If so, why? If not, why?

What different ways might there be to solve X? What might the strengths and limitations of these be? Following on, which would you choose to solve X and why?

Who might be able to solve X? Why?

Having considered our problem, what could you use to solve it?

How might you go about finding an answer to X?

What might today's learning enable us to solve/explain?

How might the problem be solved using X,Y and Z?

On the surface X appears to be a mystery – how might you try to solve it?

What clues might there be leading to a solution for X?

Where might we find a solution to X?

If you were presenting today's problems to next year's class, what would be your advice as to how to go about solving them? Why would you give this advice? How does it link to your own learning?

If part X of the problem changed, how would this affect your solution?

What might you apply to the problem in an effort to solve it?

To what might a solution to X connect? Why?

Appendix 3 – Ready-to-use Analysis Questions

Contrast and Comparison

How might X be made more like Y?

How is X different from Y?

What might have caused X to be different to Y?

Why might X and Y have developed differently over time?

How could we distinguish between X and Y?

What could we do to prove that X and Y are different/similar?

Why are X and Y not identical?

Are we able to prove that X is not Y? How?

What would have to happen for X and Y to become more/less similar/different?

How could we categorise X and Y together? How could we categorise X and Y apart?

What elements of X does Y possess (and vice versa)? What then, makes them different?

What analogy might fit both X and Y?

X is to Y, as what is to what? Can you prove it through reasoning?

How does Z's relationship to X and Y differ? Why?

What might Z and X's relationship share with Z and Y's relationship?

How might you draw out the differences/similarities of X and Y for an audience?

What events might affect X but not Y?

How do the elements which make up X and differ from those which make up Y?

How do the origins of X and Y compare?

How could X become Y in N steps?

What conditions might benefit one, but not the other, of X and Y? Why?

Where might X be found, yet not Y? Why?

Where might X and Y both flourish? Why?

How might the users of X and Y differ?

Do X and Y have certain things in common? If so, what are they and why do they have them in common?

What sort of relationship do X and Y have with one another?

How might a world without Y be different from a world without X?

How does the importance of X to human affairs differ to that of Y?

How is human engagement with X and Y different?

What is the cause of the similarities/differences between X and Y?

Can you outline the similarities and differences between X and Y?

Examine

How might you plan a thorough examination of X?

What findings might you predict prior to examining X? On what do you base your predictions?

What tools or concepts might you use to examine X?

Which tools/concepts do you feel would be of most use when examining X? Why?

What questions would you try to answer when examining X?

What key question would you use to frame your examination of X? Why?

How might your choice of framing question affect your examination of X?

How might you break X down into manageable segments to examine? What would you need to take into account when doing this? What might be the benefits and pitfalls of reducing X to constituent parts for examination?

How might two examinations of X be different?

Where might be the best place to conduct an examination of X?

How might the environment affect your examination of X?

Who might have previously examined X and how might their findings assist (or hinder) us?

Why might you examine X?

What benefits may there be from working independently/with others on an examination of X? And what potential problems might there be?

What criteria might be useful as a framework for examining X? How might you choose these criteria? How might you apply them? And what might be the effect of all this?

Can an examination of X reveal its true nature or condition? If so, how and why? If not, why not?

How might the results you gain by examining X influence your opinion?

Does the nature or condition of X change over time?

What might be the meaning or purpose of X?

What conclusions might an examination of X lead to? How might you examine whether these are true/valid/reliable?

How might different examinations of X produce different results? What might this tell us about X? What might this tell us about the nature of analysis/the examinations?

In your examination of X, was certain material implicit? Did it rely on you making judgements or inferring meaning? If so, what are the implications of this? If not, can a surface-level examination tell us the true nature or condition of X? Why?

How might you conduct an examination of X that is biased by motive Y? How might knowing this help you to be more objective?

How might X be affected by your examination?

How might examining X affect your understanding of it?

Analyse

How might you analyse X?

Can you produce an analysis of X?

Can you produce an analysis of X, paying particular attention to element Y/the influence of Y?

How might X impact on Y?

What is the structure of X?

How might you analyse the structure of X?

How might we analyse the parts that go to make up X?

What (elements) lie(s) at the heart of X?

What (elements) lie(s) behind the functioning/meaning/structure of X?

What might be the meaning of X? What has led you to that conclusion?

What might we conclude from our analysis of X?

How might we subject X to analysis?

What might you expect to find by subjecting X to analysis?

How might analyses of X differ? What implications does this have for our own analysis? What implications does this have for the knowledge of X we may claim to create?

What might we learn by comparing the results of different analyses of X?

When analysing X, what processes/tools/concepts/ideas might be useful? Why?

What method should we use to analyse X? Why? How will we judge if our method has been successful? What might we do if it proves unsuccessful?

What is central/vital/key to X? What is not particularly important to X?

How might X be used? What is it about X that lends itself to such uses?

Who? What? Where? When? Why? How? (5W's + H)

What might X be trying to communicate?

How might motive/bias have influenced X?

What might be the motives of person A?

How might person A have been led to act in this way?

Why did you behave as you did?

What might be the reasoning behind X?

How might X have come to be as it is?

What might be the constituent parts of X?

How might individual/group A's intentions have led to the development of X/situation X? What else may have caused it to develop as it did?

What might have made X like it is?

What influences X internally, what influences it externally? And what influence(s) does X have on other things?

What might be the nature of X? What evidence do you have to support this?

Question

Why X? Why X and not Y?

Why might X exist? What might have to happen for X not to exist?

Why might someone ask questions of X?

What questions might we ask about X? Why those particular questions?

What aim should we use to decide what questions to ask about X?

How might a person's motivation/bias/intention affect the questions they ask about X?

Based on your own purpose/motive/aim, what questions would you ask about X?

How might you plan your questioning of X?

What counterfactual questions might you ask about X, in order to offset your original questions?

How could we use questions to achieve a certain result? What might this tell us about the use of questions? How might we use the information to inform our future questioning?

How might the questions asked by person A and person B be different? Why? What might this tell us about the similarities and differences between them?

Would open or closed questions be more helpful to us when analysing X? Why?

How might our questions change if X could respond? (For example, if X was a person we were in contact with, as opposed to a group/idea/object etc.)

How might the situation affect the questions you ask about X? Or the answers you obtain?

What objective questions could we ask about X? What subjective questions could we ask about X? How might these questions be similar or different? What might be the use of asking questions of both types? How would our analysis differ if we favoured one type over another?

What is the overarching question framing your analysis? Why? What might be the pros and cons of beginning with such a question?

Bearing in mind what we have found out about X, how might you formulate a set of questions that someone else could use to reach similar conclusions?

Use everything you know about X to come up with a set of questions that anybody could use to analyse it?

What questions about X might we need to ask as a result of new information Y?

What assumptions do your questions rest on? What assumptions do person A's questions rest on?

Are there any questions about X that cannot be answered? If so, why can they not be answered? Can you imagine how they might be answered in the future?

How valid/reliable/generalizable are the answers to your questions? Why? How might you improve their validity/reliability/generalizability?

Under what circumstances might it be difficult to ask and answer questions about X?

Investigate

How might we investigate (the nature of) X?

How might we investigate whether what person A says is true or not?

Why might it be useful to investigate X?

Under what circumstances might it become necessary to investigate X? Why might it become necessary to investigate X?

What motives might people have for investigating X?

How might an investigation of X proceed/work/be structured?

How might an investigation of X be made relevant to our learning?

What could you use to frame your investigation of X?

How might investigating X differ from investigating Y?

How might time, place and context affect your investigation of X?

How might an investigation into a concept be different from an investigation into a physical thing?

What could you use to investigate X?

What might be the benefits of investigating X?

What might you not be allowed to do or use when investigating X?

What problems might you encounter when investigating X?

What difficulties do you think you will have to overcome when planning how to investigate X?

How might the nature of X affect any attempt to investigate it?

What might a successful investigation of X require?

What do you hope to gain by investigating X?

How might different methods of investigation affect what you can find out?

What assumptions might underpin an investigation of X?

What criteria could you use to guide your investigation? Why? Could you use these to judge your results? Why or why not?

What principles will you follow when investigating X? Why?

What question(s) will you seek to answer by investigating X?

How might you check the validity/reliability of any results you generate while investigating X?

If X changed while you were investigating it, how would you respond?

What might be the similarities and differences when investigating X and Y?

How will you judge whether your investigation has been a success or not?

Where might it be easiest to investigate X? Where might it be hardest to investigate X? Where might it be most effective to investigate X?

Appendix 4 – Ready-to-use Synthesis Questions

Create

How might X have been created?

How might you create an image/dramatization/story/poem about X?

What might an image/dramatization/story/poem about X be like?

How might X connect to Y? (Can you create a connection between X and Y?)

Could you link X to Y *and* to Z? (Can you create a connection between X, Y *and* Z?)

What conditions are needed for the creation of X? Why? Are there multiple conditions? If so, what might connect these together?

What different stories of X's origin can you tell? How do they differ? Why do they differ? Are there certain things which are common to all stories explaining the creation of X? Why?

What might X help to create?

What could you use X to create?

How might you use X to create Y/something new?

What circumstances might be needed for the creation of X? Why?

If you were to alter condition Y, would X still have been created?

Did the creation of X stifle other possible creations? What might these have looked like? How might the world be different if these, and not X, had been created first?

How might you solve problem X?

What solution(s) can you create for problem X?

Can you create X for situation Y? (For example: What might a constitution for Britain be like? Or: Can you create a constitution (X) for Britain (Y))

What motives might have been behind the creation of X?

Could you create a new/better/more streamlined/more effective/less restrictive version of X?

Can you explain the thinking behind your creation?

What consequences have come from the creation of X?

Can you create an answer to question/problem X?

What processes might be involved in the creation of X? How might these processes interact? What sort of relationship between them is necessary for the creation of X?

Does the creation of X require certain things to happen?

Does the creation of X always lead to certain effects?

Is the creation of X implicated in a chain of cause and effect? Could the creation be explained by indirect factors?

Can you create an image/story/experiment in the style of X?

What do you need to know in order to create something?

Design

How might X have been designed?

What alternative designs of X might there be?

What would an alternative to X look like?

How might you design an alternative to X/alternative version of X?

Can you design a solution to problem X?

What might be a solution to X and how would you put this into practice?

What difficulties might you encounter when designing a solution to X?

How might the design of X differ from that of Y?

What constraints might be necessary to encourage a workable design for X?

When designing X, what considerations do you need to take into account?

How might you prioritise the various requirements of the design brief?

Can you design a version of X that takes competing interests/ideas/demands into account?

If the situation changed, how would you design a response to this?

How might person A and person B design different responses to situation Y?

What influence might factor Y have on your design of a solution to problem X?

Why might X have been designed as it is?

What has influenced the design of X? Why has it?

What purposes or intentions do you think the designers of X had in mind?

What unintentional consequences has the design of X led to? What does this tell us about the design of X? What does it tell us about how people are using the design?

How might you design X so that it is future-proof?

Examine X. Use your findings to suggest how it was designed. Why do you think it was designed in this way?

How might you design X so that it is open rather than closed?

How might you redesign X?

What information would be most helpful to someone designing X? How might they get hold of this information? How might it influence their planning?

Look at X. Is there a difference between the design and the reality? Why?

What is the best way to go about designing something? What benefits are there to following a process? What drawbacks are there?

How are designs of X similar and different?

Propose

What proposals might you make for situation X?

What solution do you propose for situation X? Why?

What ideas can you propose for altering X?

How might X be altered?

How might we deal with situation X?

What ideas might individuals A and B propose in situation X? Why?

What did you use to make your proposals?

How do you propose to explain your decision?

How might we best explain the actions of person A?

Why might person A have acted as they did? What do you think motivated or caused person A's behaviour?

What theory might explain X? What theory might explain X, Y and Z?

Can you propose an alternative to that which currently exists?

Considering our discussion, what do you propose?

Based on your knowledge and understanding, what do you propose we do?

How might we maintain/analyse/critique/circumvent/challenge/delineate/infer X?

What plan do you have for situation X? How do you plan to do X?

What ideas can you offer as to why X is as it is?

What might have caused X? How? Why?

Who might be responsible for X? Why?

How might person A feel? What might have caused their feelings?

How might person A respond to X? Why might X elicit this response?

How might you improve X?

How might changes to X cause you to alter your proposals?

What factors influenced your proposals? If these were to change, how might your proposals change?

How might we solve problem X? What alternatives are there?

How might the proposal of an idea differ from the proposal of a plan?

Would problem X be better dealt with by a plan or an idea? Why?

If aspect Y of X were to change, what impact might this have on your proposals? Are certain aspects of X more important to your proposal?

Why might your proposal work? Why might it fail? Why might it address the problem? How might it fail to address the problem?

How might you improve your proposition(s)?

Why do you think your proposal will be successful? What evidence/examples/reasons do you have to support your belief?

Construct

What theory might explain the information/observations/data?

How might you theorise X from Y?

How might you construct an argument to support your point?

Can you make an argument supporting your point?

Can you construct a meaning for X?

How might you bring X, Y and Z together to form a theory?

Can you construct a new theory which takes X into account?

What might you be able to build using these concepts?

How might these concepts help us to build a model or theory explaining X?

How could we use the concepts we have learnt about to construct a theory of X?

How has person A used observations/data to construct a theory? Do you agree with their theory? Why?

What relationships and concepts are important to theory X?

What might a theory/idea connecting X and Y be like?

What might be the strengths and weaknesses of a theory that tries to explain X, Y and Z?

How can we explain the data/observations?

How could someone go about defending X?

How could someone construct an attack/critique of X?

How can we account for X?

How might person A attempt to incorporate X into their theory?

Could a theory be constructed which challenges X/fits the evidence/gives suggestions for further investigation?

Why might it be possible to construct a theory of X? Why might it not be possible to construct a theory of X?

When/where might it be useful to construct a theory about X?

What might you use to construct a theory about X?

What difficulties might you encounter when trying to theorise X?

Can you construct an answer to X using the data/your knowledge?

What foundations can we construct for our answers?

What would you use to construct an answer to X?

How might individuals A and B construct different theories of X?

What does theory X depend on? How might theory X be proved wrong?

When and how could someone construct an alternative to X? How would they do this? What might make it effective?

How might someone use X, Y and/or Z to build an argument?

Hypothesise

How might you explain X?

What might explain X? How might this explanation work?

Who might be able to explain X? Why?

What might happen if X were altered? What might happen if X were altered by means Y? What might happen if X were altered by person A?

What might happen if X was brought into contact with Y?

What hypothesis might fit the facts? What hypothesis might explain X?

What might happen in situation X? Why – what has led you to such a hypothesis?

Can you think of a hypothesis which accounts for X, Y and Z?

Why might X be as it is?

How might you improve X? Why would what you have suggested be an improvement?

What might make X better or worse? Why?

How might you explain X? Given new information Y, how might your hypothesis about X alter?

How could you test your hypothesis about X?

How could X be different?

Why/where could X be different?

Who might want to explain X? Why?

How might X be explained? How might X be explained using Y/by person A?

What might be the best course of action for achieving X? Why?

What assumptions does your hypothesis rest on?

How might your hypothesis influence how you look at X?

How could someone attempt to falsify your hypothesis?

How might a change in motivation influence your hypothesis?

How many different hypotheses might possibly explain X? What does this tell us about X? What does it tell us about proposing hypotheses?

Which hypothesis about X do you think is most likely to prove correct? Why?

How might you simplify your hypothesis?

What information do you need to prove or disprove your hypothesis?

What information might lead you to alter your hypothesis? Why? What changes will you make?

How might you develop a hypothesis that explains X?

Will you hypothesis about X be true in every situation? How could you test this?

Why might someone agree or disagree with your hypothesis about X?

How might you test your hypothesis?

Appendix 5 – Ready-to-use Evaluation Questions

Assess

How might we assess X?

What assessments of X can you make?

What is the likelihood of X doing/exhibiting behaviour Y?

How might X be improved? Why? What benefits would this bring and for who?

How important is X in the context of Y?

What value might we place on X? How might this change in different circumstances?

What internal changes could alter the value of X?

What external changes might alter the value of X?

When might X have the greatest value for person A?

In what contexts would X prove reliable or valid?

How might we assess the validity or reliability of X?

What criteria could you use to assess X? Why? How might different criteria lead to different assessments?

How might you assess X in reference to Y or Z?

How might person A and person B come to different assessments of X?

Could a set of criteria be developed that resulted in uniform assessments of X no matter who was assessing it? Why?

How might we assess whether or not X can be classed as belonging to category Y?

What would we need to know in order to confidently assess X?

What is X? How do you know? What thinking led you to that assessment?

How might we assess the impact of X on Y?

What chances are there for X being successful/failing? How might these chances be enhanced or degraded?

Do the strengths of X outweigh the benefits? Why?

If you could recreate X from scratch, what might you do differently? If nothing, why then has X proved successful?

What aspects of X are the most significant? Why?

How and why might person A and person B think differently about X?

Why might X exist?

What might be the purpose of X?

Consider what you know about the world. How might X, or the way X is used, change in the future? Why?

What circumstances might be most conducive to the success of X?

What qualities does X possess that would enable it to flourish/succeed in situation Y?

Argue

What arguments could you make in favour of X?

What arguments could you make against X?

What arguments might have been put forward in order to bring X about?

What arguments might have been put forward in an attempt to prevent X coming into existence?

Who or what might argue in favour of X? Why?

Who or what might argue against X? Why?

Consider the arguments for and against X, how do they compare? Are there things which are common to both? Do they share assumptions? Or, do they make different assumptions? In either case, what are the implications for the arguments?

On what assumptions does argument X rely?

What motives might the people proposing argument X have?

How could you rebut the arguments made against X?

How might we test argument X?

How might we falsify argument X?

What arguments about X might person A's motives lead them to make?

What might you need to know and understand about X in order to successfully argue for or against it?

How could you support your claims about X?

What evidence, examples or reasons could be used in support X?

What might be the strengths and weaknesses of argument X? Why might this be so? What might it tell us about the argument more generally?

Why might argument X be convincing?

Why might individuals or groups accept that argument X is valid? What does this tells us about those individuals or groups? What might it tell us about the motivations of those people who propose argument X?

In what circumstances might argument X prove successful? Why?

How might you support what you have just said?

Why might the evidence support the argument?

On what reasoning does argument X rely?

What steps might someone go through to build an argument around X?

What emotions or shared meanings is argument X invoking?

If the premises changed, how would this affect your argument?

What new evidence could disprove argument X?

How could you maintain your position in situation Y?

Justify

How might you justify X?

Who might seek to justify X?

How might person A justify their opinion/belief/proposal? Why might they try to justify it? What might motivate them to justify X? What factors might influence their decision to justify X? What might influence the manner in which they justify X?

When might you be able to justify X? What changes will make this no longer appropriate?

When, or why, might someone be unable to justify X?

How might you use evidence or reasoning to support your argument?

What justification is there for accepting that X is true?

How might you justify your position in the face of argument X? How might you justify your argument to person A or group B?

What impact might evidence X have on your defence of position Y?

Considering the strengths and weaknesses of the claims, which do you believe to be most justified in the circumstances?

How might you assess the justifications put forward for position X?

How might you justify a change to/maintenance of the status quo?

When could the use of X be justified?

Where might the use of X be justified?

In what circumstances might you try to justify X?

How might you prove that X is either right or reasonable?

Is there any evidence to justify X? Could you manufacture evidence to justify X? How?

What underpins your justification? What underpins person A's justification?

Can you critique person A's justification by analysing the logical/deductive/semantic/theoretical grounds on which it is based?

How has person A tried to justify their reasoning/position/actions?

To what, or to who, does person A appeal when justifying their position?

How might an emotional justification of X be different from a rational justification?

How might you justify X without using language/certain words/gesticulations/empirical evidence/logic?

How might religious and scientific/historical and philosophical/social and cultural justifications differ?

What assumptions might underlie the justification of X?

What might be the ethical/political/social/theoretical consequences of justifying X?

How might person A attempt to justify the actions of person B or group C? Why might they do this?

How might person A try to persuade other people that their justification is valid?

How can we test whether your justification of X is true or not?

Judge

What is your opinion of X? Why? What has led you to that view? What assumptions underpin it? How has your opinion been influenced by X/preconceptions/prior knowledge?

Would X or Y be better/more appropriate/more useful in situation Z?

How can we judge X?

How might person A judge X? How and why might this judgement differ from that of person B?

How might context affect someone's judgement of X?

Who might need/desire/wish to judge X?

What judgements can we make about X?

Based on the criteria, what is your opinion of X? Why?

What criteria can you use to judge X?

What is your opinion of X? On what criteria is your judgement based?

What might make it possible to judge X? Could X be judged differently according to different assumptions/demands/ideas?

What type of judgement might be of most use in situation X? Why?

Following new information Y, has your opinion of X altered? Why?

On what do your opinions about X rest? Are there motives/principles/intuitions/reasons guiding your judgements? If so, why are these important? On analysis, *are they important*?

What might be the value of X to person A/in situation B?

What are your thoughts about X?

Why might X be better than Y? And vice versa? In your opinion, which is better? Why? Will this always be the case?

Which of these ideas might be better in situation X/for group Y?

How effective is X? How have you come to that judgement? How else might we judge the effectiveness of X? What consequences does this have for our understanding of X?

What is good/bad/useful/tasteless about X? Why?

Having heard all the evidence, what is your opinion of X? How does your opinion link to the evidence? Does the evidence structure/support/negate it?

In your opinion, how might X be improved/altered/remade? What led you to such a judgement? On making your thinking clearer, does your opinion alter? Why?

X or Y? For what reasons? And these reasons – what underpins them? What work might concepts be doing in your thinking? If you were to judge the validity of your concepts, might this lead you to alter your original view? Why?

Is X justified? Why?

How might you come to form an opinion? What concepts or processes might be influential in your thinking?

Where or when might someone's judgement of X alter?

How would you prioritise the various criteria when making a judgement about X?

Critique

How might you critique X?

Can you offer us a critique of X?

How might someone critically evaluate X?

What criticisms of X are there?

How might someone go about criticising X?

What are the strengths and weaknesses of X?

Thinking critically, what is your final judgement about X?

How might person A critique X? How might this differ from your own critique? How might you explain this difference?

What relationship might there be between a person's motivation/purpose/aims and their critique of X?

How might someone use their critique of X? How might you use someone else's critique of X?

What rules do people follow when critiquing something? Do these differ depending on what is being critiqued?

What problems might arise from X? What problems might X entail? How might X be a problem? What might X make difficult?

What faults or difficulties might someone find with X?

How useful might X be? Why?

What use might X be in situation Y? Why?

What limitations does X have?

What are the causes of X's limitations?

What might be the positives and negatives/pros and cons of X?

Having analysed the positives and negatives of X, what is your opinion of it?

What criticisms of X might person A put forward?

How might someone use Y to critique X?

On what might a critique of X rely?

What do you need to know or understand in order for your critique of X to be effective?

On what criteria does your critique of X rely? How might these direct your thinking on the issue?

What could you use to critique X?

What might a critique of X entail?

On what grounds might we be able to go ahead with a critique of X?

Why might X prove difficult to critique? What, if anything, might allow us to successfully critique X?

How or why might something prove to be difficult to critique? How or why might person A struggle to critique X?

17577783R00126

Printed in Great Britain
by Amazon